JESUS

THE UNAUTHORIZED VERSION

JESUS

THE UNAUTHORIZED VERSION

EDITED AND INTRODUCED BY

MIAN RIDGE

NEW AMERICAN LIBRARY

NEW AMERICAN LIBRARY
Published by New American Library, a division of
Penguin Group (USA) Inc., 375 Hudson Street,
New York, New York 10014, USA
Penguin Group (Canada), 90 Eglinton Avenue East, Suite 700, Toronto,
Ontario M4P 2Y3, Canada (a division of Pearson Penguin Canada Inc.)
Penguin Books Ltd., 80 Strand, London WC2R 0RL, England
Penguin Ireland, 25 St. Stephen's Green, Dublin 2,
Ireland (a division of Penguin Books Ltd.)
Penguin Group (Australia), 250 Camberwell Road, Camberwell, Victoria 3124,
Australia (a division of Pearson Australia Group Pty. Ltd.)
Penguin Books India Pvt. Ltd., 11 Community Centre, Panchsheel Park,
New Delhi - 110 017, India
Penguin Group (NZ), cnr Airborne and Rosedale Roads, Albany,
Auckland 1310, New Zealand (a division of Pearson New Zealand Ltd.)
Penguin Books (South Africa) (Pty.) Ltd., 24 Sturdee Avenue,
Rosebank, Johannesburg 2196, South Africa

Penguin Books Ltd., Registered Offices:
80 Strand, London WC2R 0RL, England

Published by New American Library, a division of Penguin Group (USA) Inc.
This is an authorized reprint of a mass market edition published by Profile Books Ltd.
For information address Profile Books Ltd., 3a Exmouth House, Pine Street,
Exmouth Market, London EC1R 0JH.

First New American Library Printing, January 2007
1 3 5 7 9 10 8 6 4 2

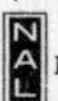

REGISTERED TRADEMARK—MARCA REGISTRADA

Set in Adobe Caslon • *Designed by Elke Sigal*
Printed in the United States of America

CONTENTS

INTRODUCTION

In December 1945, Muhammad Ali, an Egyptian peasant, was gathering *sabakh*, a rich soil that he spread over his fields, near the town of Nag Hammadi, in upper Egypt. Digging at the foot of a huge cliff, the Jabal al-Tarif, he came across a large boulder, and, buried beneath it, an old earthenware jar. His anxiety that the jar might contain a *jinn*—or spirit—was exceeded by his hope that it was filled with gold, for an ancient burial site was nearby. Ali smashed open the jar—and found over a dozen old books, bound in shriveled brown leather. He carried them home, and dumped them in the courtyard of his house. Days later his mother tore pages from some of the books and used them to light a fire.

Other pages were ripped out and sold to Ali's neighbors, or bartered for cigarettes. But eventually the books wound up in the Coptic Museum in Old Cairo. There, experts established that the books, thirteen of them, contained ancient sheets of papyrus. The papyrus bindings were dated to around A.D. 350, but the fifty-two different writings that lay within the books, written in Coptic, were even older. All had been translated from Greek, the language in which the books of the New Testament were written.

When scholars started to study the books, they were amazed to find that they were reading lost gospels from the earliest years of the Church. Not all the texts were Christian; the books also contained, for example, a copy of Plato's *Republic*. But here, among many others, were the gospels of Thomas and Philip—or so they claimed to be—and also the compellingly titled Gospel of Truth, alongside the "Secret Books" of James and John. No less than the evangelists of the New Testament, the writers of the texts found near Nag Hammadi claimed to be inspired by Jesus and to tell the truth. Yet the message—or rather messages—offered by these books was very different from the teachings of the Bible. Here were sayings of Jesus that had never been heard before—some of them bewilderingly enigmatic. God was described in unfamiliar, female terms, and one gospel purported to have been written by Jesus's "twin brother."

Then there were the portrayals of Mary Magdalene. In the Bible, she says very little; in the Nag Hammadi books, she is a commanding, authoritative woman, clever and articulate, and invariably a step ahead of Jesus's male disciples. More than once, she is described outsmarting Peter, whom the Roman Catholic Church regards as the spiritual forebear to its popes. And, unlike in any of the gospels in the Bible, she is described, in the Gospel of Philip, as "the companion of the Savior," a reference upon which the plot of Dan Brown's bestselling *The Da Vinci Code* turns. Perhaps most remarkably, in some of the newfound texts the death and resurrection of Jesus are not mentioned at all, while in others these most fundamental of Christian doctrines are roundly dismissed as untrue, naive, and simplistic.

The Nag Hammadi Library, as the collection of books became known, was not translated into English, or made widely available, until the 1970s. When they finally emerged to a wider audience, people were amazed by what they read. Here were books, written by self-confessed Christians, in the earliest years of Christianity, that bore little resemblance to the texts contained in the Bible.

But these books called themselves gospels and claimed to transmit the sayings and the teachings of Jesus. Why, then, were their contents so dramatically different from the familiar four gospels of the Bible? Did these books hold truths that had been lost—or concealed—from Christians for hundreds of years? Did, in fact, the discovery of these lost gospels threaten the rigid beliefs that had been held by Christians for two millennia?

Theologians had always known that there were disagreements in the early Church about the events of Jesus's life and death, and what Christians should make of them. Jesus left behind no writings, and nothing resembling a recitable creed. He had wandered preaching through the fishing villages on the Sea of Galilee in northern Palestine for only two or three years before he was crucified. No record of him survived in any diary or letter composed during his lifetime. Three decades after his death, still no one had sat down to write his life story; or if they had, their writings have not survived.

And yet, within one hundred years of Jesus's death, a new religion, founded on belief in Jesus as God, had spread from fishing villages in a region on the margins of the Roman Empire to Rome itself. Within three hundred years of his death, it had been adopted as the religion of the empire. During those centuries, the early Christians had succeeded in organizing themselves despite some staggeringly tough obstacles. They were persecuted, most viciously in Rome, where many were martyred. Meanwhile, they cut and pasted many disparate and contradictory versions of Jesus's story, omitting some, including others, into a uniform and disciplined Christian religion.

That they achieved any success at all can be largely attributed to Paul, the first known Christian writer. A Jew from Tarsus in eastern Turkey, Paul—then named Saul—was traveling to Damascus, or so the Bible tells us, when he was struck down by a vision of Jesus that temporarily blinded him and permanently converted him to a life of tireless proselytizing. He traveled throughout the Roman Empire, networking furiously, planting churches and insisting that the Gentiles had as much claim to membership of God's people as the Jews—thereby ensuring that Christianity became much more than a Jewish sect. And everywhere he went, Paul preached the importance of unity in the face of "strife, seditions, heresies" (Galatians 5:19–21).

Paul produced the first known Christian writings in around A.D. 50. According to his letters—without which little would be known about the earliest years of Christianity—Jesus was already being worshipped as divine. They opened the floodgates: after Paul's letters, there was an outpouring of literature as the early Christians started to record the memories of Jesus that had circulated among them for years.

Among the earliest accounts of Jesus's life were the four gospels that would later become part of the New Testament. First was the Gospel of Mark—an unknown figure believed to have been a follower of a follower of Jesus—in around A.D. 65–70. A book written by an anonymous Christian, later named Matthew, and the Gospel of Luke, who may or may not have been a physician, were written between fifteen and twenty years later. These books drew heavily on the story told by Mark. The Gospel of John is often attributed to the disciple of that name, though it was probably not finished much before A.D. 110, when John would have been long dead. At the time these books were written, it was common practice to write under another person's name. Indeed, some theologians now think Paul may have written only seven of his thirteen supposed letters.

If these were the earliest—or, at least, among the earliest—accounts of Jesus's life and teachings, a torrent of alternative versions soon followed. Indeed, Luke, who is also believed to be the author of Acts, in which he describes his missionary journeys with Paul, seems to nod to some of the authors of these alternative versions at the beginning of his gospel. "Many have undertaken to draw up an account of the things that have been fulfilled among us," he writes, "just as they were handed down to us by those who from the first were eyewitnesses and servants of the word."

If there were numerous gospels from this time, why were only four embraced by the Church? Some of these "accounts" must have contradicted Christianity's emerging orthodox (from the Greek *orthos* and *doxa*, literally "straight thinking") beliefs. In fact, it could hardly have been otherwise. In the first centuries A.D., confusion raged about who, or rather what, Jesus was. How could he be, as Paul had implied, both God and man? If he was God, what, then, was his relationship with his father, who was also God? By the end of the first century, many Christians believed that Jesus was a divine spirit who merely adopted a human form for his ministry. Later, others were to teach that he was not actually, or not completely, divine. Pending the emergence of an efficient means of settling these questions, the early Church contained very different, even radically opposed, beliefs. One of the earliest examples of its efforts to achieve consensus was the last testament of Ignatius, Bishop of Antioch, written shortly before he was torn apart by animals in the Colosseum in Rome between A.D. 107 and 117. On his way to his martyrdom, Ignatius wrote a series of letters to churches in Asia Minor and Rome. Jesus, he wrote in one of them, "was truly born and ate and drank, was truly persecuted under Pontius Pilate [and] was truly raised from the dead." Perhaps his own looming fate gave strength to this conviction; for a man anticipating an excruciating death, the belief that Jesus had also suffered as a man must have offered some comfort. As Christianity spread, and persecution against Christians rose, it became increasingly important for Christians to formulate a definitive doctrine of Jesus as God incarnate.

And so they did. The intellectuals of the early Church drew on the Greek philosophical tradition and the gospels, particularly John's, to formulate the doctrine of Jesus that Christians proclaim today: that Jesus was both God and man and of the "same being" as the father. In the process, they intensified the insistency with which they claimed that the four gospels of Matthew, Mark, Luke, and John were the only true accounts of the life of Jesus.

One of the earliest and most explicit endorsements of these four—and only these four—gospels was made by Irenaeus, Bishop of Lyon, in Gaul, now France. In his book *Against Heresies*, in A.D. 180, Irenaeus wrote that "the gospels could not possibly be more or less in number than they are" because they could be traced back to the disciples. But Irenaeus was less interested in proving this connection—something few modern theologians would attempt—than in denigrating the alternative gospels. Some Christians, he wrote, "boast that they have more gospels than there really are . . . but really they have no gospel which is not full of blasphemy." One of the gospels that he singled out for scorn was a text that caught the eye of the first scholars to see the Nag Hammadi texts: the Gospel of Truth.

After two thousand years of Christianity, it is easy to define heresy as whatever contradicts Church doctrine. But in the early years, when doctrinal battles were still being fought, this was a vexed distinction. Originally, "heresy," from the Greek word for "choice" (or "difference"), simply meant a "sect" or "faction." Irenaeus might have condemned certain teachings as heretical, but he did so with force only because they had gained some ground among Christians. Indeed, the "heretic" to whom Irenaeus attributed the Gospel of Truth, Valentinus, was a Christian leader who very nearly became the Bishop of Rome.

Few of Valentinus's writings have survived, but we know that he was educated in Alexandria, an important center of Hellenistic and Christian thought. His followers claimed he was a follower of Theudas, a Christian teacher who was said to be a disciple of Paul. In around A.D. 136, Valentinus went to Rome, where, according to one contemporary writer—no follower of his, but an orthodox Church leader called Tertullian—he narrowly missed getting what was to become the top job. Had he done so, one of the earliest and most virulent heresies of the early Church, known as Gnosticism, might have been enshrined as orthodox Christianity.

Valentinus was no fifth columnist of the early

Church. He considered himself a devoted—and no doubt orthodox—Christian. Valentinus had many followers, who also called themselves Christians. The Gospel of Truth, which he may indeed have written, is a lyrical meditation on the love of God. Yet this text rests on beliefs very different from those now associated with the earliest followers of Jesus.

Valentinus was one of the foremost proponents of a mystical belief in the possibility of salvation through attainment of a divine message, or special knowledge. This belief was later called Gnosticism—after the Greek word *gnosis*, meaning "knowledge"—and was less a religious movement than an approach adopted by a number of sects that proliferated around the Mediterranean Sea and in Central Asia during the first centuries A.D.

Most Gnostics, including Valentinus, believed in the existence of a pure spirit world, and a corrupt material world—from which man, though originally divine, had become separated. Gnostic Christians like Valentinus believed that Jesus had been sent from the spirit world to impart the knowledge—gnosis—which would enable men to return to their spiritual home. In descending to the world of flesh, Jesus had a divine precedent: an ethereal power, or aeon, called Sophia ("wisdom" in Greek), whose separation from the spirit world had brought the material world into being. Key to this belief—so unlike Christian orthodoxy—was its stress on initiation and exclusivity: only a select few could reach the high world, the *pleroma* (or "fullness" in Greek).

No one knows the exact origins of Gnosticism—though some have claimed it arose out of Judaism, or Greek mythology, or both, as well as other traditions. Irenaeus believed that Christian Gnosticism began with "the father of all heretics," Simon Magus. Magus may be the Simon described briefly in Acts: a magician who "amazed the nation of Samaria, saying that he himself was someone great." An entertaining account of him is found in *Apologies*, a theological work written by Justin Martyr, a leader of the early Church. He describes Simon as a maverick who can levitate and fly. His companion is Helene, a prostitute he rescued from a brothel in the Phoenician city of Tyre, believing her to be an incarnation of Sophia. In an earlier life she was Helen of Troy.

And yet, such entertainments aside, it is clear that the early Christian Church was widely affected by Gnostic beliefs. Many of the texts found at Nag Hammadi are, to varying degrees, peppered with Gnostic language, alluding to things "hidden" and "secret," even referring to the *pleroma* and to Sophia.

This emphasis on things sacred and hidden is of a completely different order to that which survives in orthodox Christianity. Andrew Welburn, in *The Beginnings of Christianity*, describes many passages in the New Testament gospels in which Jesus teaches his disciples things that are withheld from the wider community. He instructs his disciples "apart," referring to "outsiders" and "insiders" and "the mystery of the kingdom of God." Yet in most Gnostic literature, secrecy is the dominant theme: in some Gnostic books, Jesus's teachings are so tortuously complicated that their meaning is effectively hidden.

Irenaeus and other Christians like him did not appreciate the exclusivity implicit in this at all. He believed that Jesus had come to save all people, not the few, and that his message should be universally accessible. Neither was this the only thing Irenaeus disliked about the teachings of men such as Valentinus. A Gnostic view of Jesus could lead Christians to reject the most fundamental of Christian beliefs: the redeeming power of Jesus's death and resurrection.

In the Bible, Jesus's disciples come to understand their Savior's role in terms of his death and resurrection. To Gnostics, knowledge alone was salvation. Since his physical death and resurrection were not essential to the Gnostic view of redemption, Jesus did not have to be a man; indeed, better that he was not, the material world being a corrupt creation. To many Gnostics, despite his descent to earth bringing gnosis, Jesus was never quite human.

The Second Treatise of the Great Seth, a book in the Nag Hammadi Library, mocks those who believe that the death and resurrection of Jesus are important: for they "proclaim the doctrine of a dead man." In the Acts of John, a book with many Gnostic passages, Jesus is described appearing in another place while he is apparently being crucified, or laughing on the cross. In the

Apocalypse of Peter, another Nag Hammadi text, Jesus warns Peter to beware of those who "will cleave to the name of a dead man." Lest there be any doubt who he is talking about, he specifically mentions "bishops and also deacons . . . these people are dry canals."

As if their denial of Jesus's humanity was not abhorrent enough to the orthodox Church, some of the Gnostics held even more appalling views. They argued that though Jesus was a divine guide, helping his followers toward gnosis, he was not, strictly speaking, essential to the process. In the texts of such Gnostics, Jesus teaches that gnosis is hidden within the individual; it needs no divine intercession to uncover it. To know oneself, according to these pure Gnostics, is to know God.

Of all the texts found near Nag Hammadi, it is the Gospel of Thomas that has caused the most excitement. A fragment of it had been found in 1896, when two British archaeologists, rummaging through a heap of ancient rubbish in the ancient Egyptian town of Oxyrhynchus, beside the River Nile, found a sheet of papyrus. This contained eight "sayings of our Lord."

In 1904, two more fragments were found. Tantalizingly, with many missing words, one of these pages read: "These are the [. . .] sayings [. . .] the living Jesus spoke [. . .] also called Thomas. [. . .]" Half a century later, theologians were able to read the full 114 chapters of the gospel that claimed to be written by Didymus Judas Thomas: Jesus's twin brother, according to one legend. "Didymus" and "Thomas" both mean "twin," in Greek and Aramaic, respectively. (It is also claimed that another of the Nag Hammadi texts, the Book of St. Thomas the Contender, was written by Jesus's twin.)

Probably written in Syria, the Gospel of Thomas is thought to be among the oldest of the Nag Hammadi books. Many theologians believe that although it was probably written in the second century, the Gospel of Thomas may contain sayings from the first century. Some theologians go further, believing it contains sayings that go back to Jesus himself and that it should be inserted into the Bible as the "fifth gospel."

Unlike the biblical gospels, Thomas's gospel contains no narrative of Jesus's life or passion, only "secret sayings." Some of these are, in fact, similar to words spoken by Jesus in the biblical gospels; others are entirely different. Of these, some have a Gnostic character. Instead of being presented as a Savior of man in his life, death, and resurrection, Jesus dispenses wisdom, by telling his followers that God is to be found in themselves. Thus, for example, he says: "the kingdom is inside of you, and it is outside of you. When you come to know yourselves, then you will become known, and you will realize that it is you who are the sons of the living father." And a little later, "There is light within a man of light, and he lights up the whole world. If he does not shine, he is darkness."

Elaine Pagels, in *Beyond Belief*, argues intriguingly that the biblical gospel of John was written to refute the teachings of the Gospel of Thomas. Thus, John contains the lines, "I am the light of the world" and "whoever does not come to me walks in darkness." The meaning of this seems clear: for the writer of John, the light of salvation resides not in man but in Jesus's ministry. Pagels also suggests that the book's attribution to Jesus's twin is a symbolic device; that is, once an individual knows himself, he becomes as one with Jesus.

Theologians had studied the Christian Gnostics before the Nag Hammadi discoveries, through the writings of heresy hunters like Irenaeus. In addition, a couple of Gnostic texts were discovered in the late eighteenth century and during the nineteenth century, but these were not widely published until after the Nag Hammadi discoveries found fame. This sudden—and previously unimagined—glut of early scriptures has provided evidence of many new Gnostic ideas, including some striking new portrayals of familiar characters from the New Testament. Perhaps the most startling of these concern the always-fascinating figure of Mary Magdalene.

In the sixth century—half a millennium after her death—Mary Magdalene abruptly became a prostitute, at least as far as the Church was concerned. The reason was a sermon given by Pope Gregory the Great, in which he confused her with the fallen woman described in chapter 7 of the Gospel of Luke. The association stuck, and Mary Magdalene—who in fact plays rather a quiet role in the biblical gospels—assumed a gritty glamour, exciting both pity and sexual fantasy, both of which are evident in the many sensuous paintings made of her. In the sixteenth century, Titian depicted her naked, with long, flowing hair covering much of her body but not her breasts. In Frederick Sandys's mid-nineteenth-century, pre-Raphaelite portrait, Mary Magdalene is clothed, but she seems to be straining out of her dress, flushed, her scarlet lips parted.

In the Bible, although she does not say very much, Mary Magdalene is clearly an important figure: in the Gospel of John it is she who discovers that Jesus has risen from the dead and first speaks to him. But this is a walk-on role compared to her great prominence in noncanonical gospels, one of which, indeed, is attributed to her. The Gospel of Mary, which is thought to date from the second half of the second century, survives in three incomplete manuscripts, including one in the Nag Hammadi Library. Part of this gospel was discovered in Cairo in 1896; another fragment was unearthed in the Oxyrhynchus excavations. In this gospel Mary Magdalene is more intelligent and courageous than Jesus's disciples. She also deals gracefully with a belligerent Peter, who sometimes refuses to listen to her. Interestingly, a similar relationship is described in the Gospel of Thomas and in the Pistis Sophia (Faith Wisdom), a third- or fourth-century text discovered in 1773.

Could this impressive woman be closer to the real

Mary Magdalene—assuming she existed—than the woman described in the Bible? Some theologians have speculated that the New Testament deliberately downplayed her importance to Jesus's ministry in favor of the disciples, and especially Peter. It is more likely that the tensions between Mary and Peter reflect disagreements in the second-century Church over the role of women. Yet Christian feminists should pause, and reflect, before they rush to embrace Gnosticism. At the end of the Gospel of Thomas, Peter asks Jesus to "make Mary leave us because females are not worthy of life"; Jesus responds by saying that he will give her a sex change—"make her male" (he does not say how). This may reflect the Gnostic belief that women represent the material world and men the spiritual.

Recently, *The Da Vinci Code* has generated fresh interest in Mary Magdalene's relationship with Jesus. The Gospel of Philip, another Gnostic text discovered at Nag Hammadi, hints at a sexual relationship between the two. Shortly after describing Mary Magdalene as Jesus's "companion," this gospel says that "Christ loved her more than all the disciples and used to kiss her often on the [. . .]." The last word has been lost, but translators often insert the word "mouth." In the Gospel of Mary, moreover, Peter tells her that ". . . we know that the Savior loved you more than the rest of women." It is just about possible that these gospels preserved memories of a relationship between Jesus and Mary that the authors of the biblical gospels chose to forget. Yet nowhere in the Gnostic gospels is it said that this was a sexual relationship; in other gospels kissing signified spiritual closeness. These books do proclaim, nevertheless, that Jesus had the greatest respect and admiration for Mary Magdalene, and that he loved her.

We do not know whether Irenaeus was familiar with the Gospel of Mary. Had he known Mary's gospel, presumably he would have denounced it too, along with every other Gnostic book or gospel other than those of the four evangelists.

As the Church emerged, this view became enshrined. In A.D. 312, Emperor Constantine converted to Christianity—giving the bishops much greater control over the Church. A few years later, in A.D. 367, Athanasius, Bishop of Alexandria, wrote his customary Easter letter to the churches and monasteries under his jurisdiction. In it he provided what is believed to be the first recorded list of the twenty-seven books of the New Testament as it exists today: with four gospels and twenty-three other writings. He also issued a diatribe against heretics and their "apocryphal books to which they attribute antiquity and give the name of saints." His aim, we may assume, was that such writings would be destroyed, and their teachings with them.

It was around this time that the Nag Hammadi texts were buried. Not far from where they were found is a monastery, St. Pachomius. The monks of St. Pachomius would have received Athanasius's epistle. Perhaps, shortly after reading it, a hooded figure hurried from the monastery toward the Jabal al-Tarif, carrying a heavy earthenware jar.

A millennium and a half after they were buried, the ancient manuscripts found at Nag Hammadi lie under glass in the Coptic Museum in Cairo. Soon, another Gnostic text will be displayed with them: the Gospel of Judas, which was published in April 2006. Like the Nag Hammadi discoveries, the Gospel of Judas was written in Coptic and had been translated from the Greek. It too was bound in a book that contained other Gnostic writings, among them the First Apocalypse of James, part of the Nag Hammadi Library. Discovered in a cave in the desert near El Minya, in Egypt, in the 1970s, the manuscript circulated for years between antiquities dealers before it arrived at the Maecenas Foundation for Ancient Art in Switzerland. There, scholars set about restoring and translating the badly damaged text—the only known version of this gospel—which had broken into a thousand fragments.

The contents of this book were as startling as the stories found at Nag Hammadi—little wonder Irenaeus had condemned this very gospel, in A.D. 180, as "fictitious."

In the Bible, a venal Judas Iscariot betrays Jesus, accepting thirty pieces of silver to turn him over to the authorities, who crucified him. For two thousand years the figure of Judas has been reviled, his name used to insult those suspected of treachery. But in this gospel, Judas is Jesus's most faithful friend and the only disciple who fully understands his master. He only betrays Jesus because Jesus asks him to. Jesus's desire for death here is typically Gnostic: he wants his spirit to be freed from his body.

Ostensibly at least, the early Church embraced the four gospels of the Bible, partly because it thought they had been written by people who knew Jesus, or were close to his disciples. Modern theologians are less certain of this. Yet these gospels, of the many alternatives, were perhaps also the most effective scriptural basis for the emerging Church. Their portrayal of Jesus as God-made-man, in whose suffering lay salvation, must have served as inspiration for persecuted Christians. And, in an oral society, the stories they contained were pleasing to tell and to hear.

But the four gospels also left huge gaps in the biography of Jesus, including his childhood. These omissions the writers of many unauthorized gospels sought to fill. Unlike the texts discovered at Nag Hammadi, most of these books have been known about, and at various times republished, since they were written. They have traditionally been referred to as the Christian "apocrypha," from the Greek for "hidden books." Less sophisticated than the Gnostic gospels and refreshingly short on abstract theology, these noncanonical gospels brim with human drama and miracles. The Church regarded them as superfluous to the canon, largely because they tended to be fanciful and late, rather than especially unorthodox. And yet several of them have had a profound effect on the beliefs of Christians and upon Church doctrine.

Mary's perpetual virginity—a long-held belief of the Roman Catholic Church—makes its first appearance in one such book, the Proto-Gospel of James, thought to have been written in the middle of the second century. Some might consider it ironic that a book that insists upon Mary's perpetual virginity should be attributed to James, believed to be the brother of Jesus. According to the Bible's Gospel of Matthew, Jesus had four brothers: James, Joseph, Simon, and Judas. The Proto-Gospel of James explains this away by claiming that Joseph already had children. The Church did not like this solution; it preferred to teach that Jesus's brothers were his cousins.

The fourth- or fifth-century History of Joseph the Carpenter elaborates further: when Mary moves into Joseph's house, and finds Joseph's son James "hearted broke and sad on account of the loss of his mother," she brings him up as her own.

The Proto-Gospel of James also describes Mary's presentation in the temple when she was a child: a feast in the Roman Catholic and Orthodox churches. Mary's bodily assumption into heaven, a doctrine in the Roman Catholic Church, is another nonbiblical story, described in a fourth-century book.

The most entertaining stories from these gospels describe Jesus as a child. In one he is a superhuman enfant terrible who kills and cripples his enemies. Two noncanonical gospels focus on his death and resurrection: the Gospel of Nicodemus describes, in some detail, Jesus's descent into hell to rescue his Old Testament ancestors, while the Gospel of Peter describes an event the biblical gospel writers left mysterious: the resurrection.

After Constantine's conversion, the Gnostics stood little chance of survival. They seem to have disappeared in the West by the fourth century; in the East there were still Gnostic sects in the seventh century. A form of Gnosticism resurfaced during the Middle Ages in the shape of the Cathari, rebel Christians who believed that Jesus was a spirit in a human body, until Pope Innocent III efficiently slaughtered them in the thirteenth century.

One ancient sect of Gnostics, however, still exists, in southern Iraq. The Mandaeans follow the teachings of John the Baptist and practice repeated baptisms. Their language, Mandaic, is a form of Aramaic, the language spoken by Jesus: *manda* is Aramaic for "knowledge." Today, fewer than fifty thousand Mandaeans remain, but, since the war in Iraq, tens of thousands are believed to have left the country; many have reported that Islamic extremists are targeting their community. Mandaeans must marry within their own religion, and conversion to the faith is not allowed. With a sparsely scattered diaspora, they may not survive for much longer.

KEY DATES

c. A.D. 1	Jesus is born
A.D. 26–30	Saul of Tarsus (later named Paul), a Jew, comes to believe that Jesus is the Messiah
c. A.D. 30	Jesus is crucified
c. A.D. 50	Paul produces the first known Christian writings
A.D. 64	Great fire in Rome. Nero blames and executes Christians
A.D. 60–65	Paul dies
A.D. 60–68	Peter dies
A.D. 65–70	The Gospel of Mark
A.D. 66–70	Jewish revolt against Rome, ending in the destruction of Jerusalem
A.D. 80–90	The Gospels of Matthew and Luke
A.D. 90–110	The Gospel of John
A.D. 90–150	The Gospel of Thomas
A.D. 107–117	Ignatius, Bishop of Antioch, is martyred in the Colosseum in Rome
A.D. 100–180	The Gospel of Truth
A.D. 100–200	The Gospel of Mary, the Secret Book of John, the Secret Book of James, and other "Gnostic" books

c. A.D. 150	The Proto-Gospel of James and the Gospel of Peter; not especially unorthodox books, later left out of the Bible
A.D. 180	Irenaeus, Bishop of Lyon, writes *Against Heresies*, in which he says there can be only four gospels—Matthew, Mark, Luke, and John—and condemns heretical writings, including the Gospel of Truth
A.D. 249–251	Major persecution of Christians under Emperor Decius
A.D. 312	Emperor Constantine becomes a Christian
A.D. 321	Constantine decrees Sunday the official day of rest for Roman Christians
A.D. 325	The first general council of the Church, at Nicaea, agrees that Jesus is fully human and fully divine
A.D. 367	Athanasius, Bishop of Alexandria, condemns heretical writings in his Easter letter
A.D. 382	Pope Damasus authorizes a complete text of the books of the Bible
c. A.D. 400	A collection of gospels is buried near Nag Hammadi. Among them are the Gospel of Thomas and the Gospel of Truth, the Secret Books of John and James, and the Gospel of Mary

ONE

Jesus's Parents

"Mary I called Mother; Joseph, Father"

Mary and Joseph, the mother and guardian of Jesus, are among the most iconic figures in Christianity. Mary has a role second only to Jesus: the most painted woman in history, she inspires the devotion and prayers of hundreds of millions. But the Bible tells us little about her life, or that of Joseph, her husband. In the earliest gospel, Mark, Mary is mentioned only once by name. And although the other gospels, written a few years later, make more of her, Mary is hardly referred to after Jesus's birth. None of the books of the Bible gives details of her birth or death. Biographical information about Joseph in the Bible is even scarcer.

Later gospels, written to fill this gap, do so richly, and many of the stories have been woven into the rituals and beliefs of the Eastern and Western Churches—particularly those about Jesus's mother. The oldest text containing stories of the early life of Mary is the Proto-Gospel of James. The book was especially influential in the development of the veneration of Mary.

The Proto-Gospel of James introduces Mary's parents, Anna and Ioachim (sometimes called Joachim), who were later made into saints and featured prominently in the art of the Middle Ages. St. Anne was especially popular: by the fourteenth century a number of European churches claimed to possess relics of her bones. In addition, the Proto-Gospel of James tells the story of Mary being presented in the temple at the age of three, and its description of Mary being fed at the hands of an angel was often depicted by medieval artists.

Yet this book and others like it were not merely written to satisfy Christians' curiosity about Jesus's family: they had a deeper theological purpose. By elevating Mary, the Proto-Gospel of James lends weight to Jesus's divinity. By the time of the Gospel of Pseudo-Matthew, which was probably written in the fifth century, this had become a well-established literary tradition. As well as rehashing stories lifted from the Proto-Gospel of James, this gospel adds some innovations, such as the description of Mary as a young woman so saintly that she coined the expression "thanks be to God" as a salutation.

What man could be worthy of such a woman? This was a question that early Christian writers also sought to answer. In the Proto-Gospel of James, Joseph is a prosperous contractor who—extremely reluctantly—becomes Mary's guardian. His portrayal as a widower with children—a tale further embroidered by the fourth- or fifth-century History of Joseph the Carpenter—is an attempt to explain away biblical references to Jesus's siblings and bolster the idea that Mary remained a virgin for the rest of her life.

The History of Joseph the Carpenter is written as

if narrated by Jesus and ends with a long-winded description of Joseph's death at the age of 111. Joseph died, Jesus tells us, with every one of his teeth. Mary's death is described in many nonbiblical texts. One of the oldest, probably dating from the fifth century, is entitled the Book of John Concerning the Falling Asleep of Mary, in which the apostles appear at her bedside from the far corners of the world.

Noncanonical books, too, tell the story of Mary's assumption into heaven, an event that has been celebrated by the Orthodox and Roman Catholic churches for centuries. In 1950 the Roman Catholic Church enshrined the assumption as a dogma: an article of faith for Catholics.

AND behold an angel of the Lord appeared, saying unto her: "Anna, Anna, the Lord hath hearkened unto thy prayer, and thou shalt conceive and bear, and thy seed shall be spoken of in the whole world." And Anna said: "As the Lord my God liveth, if I bring forth either male or female, I will bring it for a gift unto the Lord my God, and it shall be ministering unto him all the days of its life."

And behold there came two messengers saying unto her: "Behold Ioachim thy husband cometh with his flocks: for an angel of the Lord came down unto him saying: 'Ioachim, Ioachim, the Lord God hath hearkened unto thy prayer. Get thee down hence, for behold thy wife Anna shall conceive.'" And Ioachim gat him down and called his herdsmen, saying: "Bring me hither ten lambs without blemish and without spot, and they shall be for the Lord my God; and bring me twelve tender calves, and they shall be for the priests and for the assembly of the elders; and a hundred kids for the whole people."

. . .

And her months were fulfilled, and in the ninth month Anna brought forth. And she said unto the midwife: "What have I brought forth?" And she said: "A female." And Anna said: "My soul is magnified this day," and she laid herself down. And when the days were fulfilled, Anna purified herself and gave suck to the child and called her name Mary.

And day by day the child waxed strong, and when she was six months old her mother stood her upon the ground to try if she would stand; and she walked seven steps and returned unto her bosom. And she caught her up, saying: "As the Lord my God liveth, thou shalt walk no more upon this ground, until I bring thee into the temple of the Lord." And she made a sanctuary in her bedchamber and suffered nothing common or unclean to pass through it. And she called for the daughters of the Hebrews that were undefiled, and they carried her hither and thither.

. . .

And unto the child her months were added: and the child became two years old. And Ioachim said: "Let us bring her up to the temple of the Lord that we may pay the promise which we promised; lest the Lord require it of us, and our gift become unacceptable." And Anna said: "Let us wait until the third year, that the child may not long after her father or mother." And Ioachim said: "Let us wait."

And the child became three years old, and Ioachim said: "Call for the daughters of the Hebrews that are undefiled, and let them take every one a lamp, and let them be burning, that the child turn not backward and her heart be taken captive away from the temple of the Lord." And they did so until they were gone up into the temple of the Lord.

And the priest received her and kissed her and blessed her and said: "The Lord hath magnified thy name among all generations: in thee in the latter days shall the Lord make manifest his redemption unto the children of Israel." And he made her to sit upon the third step of the altar. And the Lord put grace upon her and she danced with her feet and all the house of Israel loved her.

And her parents gat them down marveling, and

praising the Lord God because the child was not turned away backward.

And Mary was in the temple of the Lord as a dove that is nurtured: and she received food from the hand of an angel.

—*The Proto-Gospel of James*

And Mary was held in admiration by all the people of Israel; and when she was three years old, she walked with a step so mature, she spoke so perfectly, and spent her time so assiduously in the praises of God, that all were astonished at her, and wondered; and she was not reckoned a young infant, but as it were a grown-up person of thirty years old. She was so constant in prayer, and her appearance was so beautiful and glorious, that scarcely any one could look into her face. And she occupied herself constantly with her wool-work, so that she in her tender years could do all that old women were not able to do. And this was the order that she had set for herself: From the morning to the third hour she remained in prayer; from the third to the ninth she was occupied with her weaving; and from the ninth she again applied herself to prayer. She did not retire from praying until there appeared to her the angel of the Lord, from whose hand she used to receive food; and thus she became more and more perfect in the work of God. Then, when the older virgins rested from the praises of God, she did not rest at all; so that in the praises and vigils of God none were found before her, no one more learned in the wisdom of the law of God, more lowly in humility, more elegant in singing, more perfect in all virtue. She was indeed steadfast, immovable, unchangeable, and daily advancing to perfection. No one saw her angry, nor heard her speaking evil. All her speech was so full of grace, that her God was acknowledged to be in her tongue. She was always engaged in prayer and in searching the law, and she was anxious lest by any word of hers she should sin with regard to her companions. Then she was afraid lest in her laughter, or the sound of her beautiful voice, she should commit any fault, or lest, being elated, she should display any wrongdoing or haughtiness to one of her equals. She blessed God without intermission; and lest perchance, even in her salutation, she might cease from praising God; if any one saluted her, she used to answer by way of salutation: "Thanks be to God." And from her the custom first began of men saying, "Thanks be to God," when they saluted each other. She refreshed herself only with the food which she daily received from the hand of the angel; but the food which she obtained from the priests she divided among the poor. The angels of God were often seen speaking with her, and they most diligently obeyed her. If any one who was unwell touched her, the same hour he went home cured.

—*The Gospel of Pseudo-Matthew*

And when she was twelve years old, there was a council of the priests, saying: "Behold Mary is become twelve years old in the temple of the Lord. What then shall we do with her? lest she pollute the sanctuary of the Lord." And they said unto the high priest: "Thou standest over the altar of the Lord. Enter in and pray concerning her: And whatsoever the Lord shall reveal to thee, that let us do."

And the high priest took the vestment with the twelve bells and went in unto the Holy of Holies and prayed concerning her. And lo, an angel of the Lord appeared saying unto him: "Zacharias, Zacharias, go forth and assemble them that are widowers of the people, and let them bring every man a rod, and to whomsoever the Lord shall show a sign, his wife shall she be." And the heralds went forth over all the country round about Judaea, and the trumpet of the Lord sounded, and all men ran thereto.

And Joseph cast down his adze and ran to meet them, and when they were gathered together they went to the high priest and took their rods with them. And he took the rods of them all and went into the temple and prayed. And when he had finished the prayer he took the rods and went forth and gave them back to them: and there was no sign upon them. But Joseph received the last rod: and lo, a dove came forth of the rod and flew upon the head of Joseph. And the priest said unto Joseph: "Unto thee hath it fallen to take the virgin of the Lord and keep her for thyself." And Joseph refused, saying: "I have sons, and I am an old man, but she is a girl: lest I became a laughingstock to the children of Israel." And the priest said unto Joseph: "Fear the Lord thy God, and remember what things God did unto Dathan and Abiram and Korah, how the earth clave and they were swallowed up because of their gainsaying. And now fear thou, Joseph, lest it be so in thine house." And Joseph was afraid, and took her to keep her for himself. And Joseph said unto Mary: "Lo, I have received thee out of the temple of the Lord: and now do I leave thee in my house, and I go away to build my buildings and I will come again unto thee. The Lord shall watch over thee."

—*The Proto-Gospel of James*

And, indeed, it was our Lord Jesus Christ Himself who related this history to His holy disciples on the Mount of Olives, and all Joseph's labor, and the end of his days. And the holy apostles have preserved this conversation, and have left it written down in the library at Jerusalem. May their prayers preserve us! Amen.

. . .

There was a man whose name was Joseph, sprung from a family of Bethlehem, a town of Judah, and the city of King David. This same man, being well-furnished with wisdom and learning, was made a priest in the temple of the Lord. He was, besides, skillful in his trade, which was that of a carpenter; and after the manner of all men, he married a wife. Moreover, he begot for himself sons and daughters, four sons, namely, and two daughters. Now these are their names—Judas, Justus, James, and Simon. The names of the two daughters were Assia and Lydia. At length the wife of righteous Joseph, a woman intent on the divine glory in all her works, departed this life. But Joseph, that righteous man, my father after the flesh, and the spouse of my mother Mary, went away with his sons to his trade, practicing the art of a carpenter.

Now when righteous Joseph became a widower, my mother Mary, blessed, holy, and pure, was already twelve years old.

. . .

Righteous Joseph therefore received my mother, and led her away to his own house. And Mary found James the Less in his father's house, hearted broke and sad on account of the loss of his mother, and she brought him up. Hence Mary was called the mother of James. Thereafter Joseph left her at home, and went away to the shop where he wrought at his trade of a carpenter. And after the holy virgin had spent two years in his house her age was exactly fourteen years, including the time at which he received her.

. . .

At length, by increasing years, the old man arrived at a very advanced age. He did not, however, labor under any bodily weakness, nor had his sight failed, nor had any tooth perished from his mouth. In mind also, for the whole time of his life, he never wandered; but like a boy he always in his business displayed youthful vigor, and his limbs remained unimpaired, and free from all pain. His life, then, in all, amounted to one hundred and eleven years, his old age being prolonged to the utmost limit.

Now Justus and Simon, the elder sons of Joseph, were married, and had families of their own. Both the daughters were likewise married, and lived in their own houses. So there remained in Joseph's house, Judas and James the Less, and my virgin mother. I moreover dwelt along with them, not otherwise than if I had been one of his sons. But I passed all my life without fault. Mary I called my mother, and Joseph father, and I obeyed them in all that they said; nor did I ever contend against them, but complied with their commands, as other men whom earth produces are wont to do; nor did I at any time arouse their anger, or give any word or answer in opposition to them. On the contrary, I cherished them with great love, like the pupil of my eye.

It came to pass, after these things, that the death of that old man, the pious Joseph, and his departure from this world, were approaching, as happens to other men who owe their origin to this earth. And as his body was verging on dissolution, an angel of the Lord informed him that his death was now close at hand.

. . .

It came to pass thereafter, when he returned to his own house in the city of Nazareth, that he was seized by disease, and had to keep his bed. And it was at this time that he died, according to the destiny of all mankind. For this disease was very heavy upon him, and he had never been ill, as he now was, from the day of his birth. And thus assuredly it pleased Christ to order the destiny of righteous Joseph. He lived forty years unmarried; thereafter his wife remained under his care forty-nine years, and then died. And a year after her death, my mother, the blessed Mary, was entrusted to him by the priests, that he should keep her until the time of her marriage.

. . .

And I saw that death now had dominion over him. And my mother, virgin undefiled, rose and came to me, saying: "O my beloved son, this pious old man Joseph is now dying." And I answered: "O my dearest mother, assuredly upon all creatures produced in this world the same necessity of death lies; for death holds sway over the whole human race. Even thou, O my virgin mother, must look for the same end of life as other mortals. And yet thy death, as also the death of this pious man, is not death, but life enduring to eternity. Nay more, even I must die, as concerns the body which I have received from thee. But rise, O my venerable mother, and go in to Joseph, that blessed old man, in order that thou mayst see what will happen as his soul ascends from his body."

My undefiled mother Mary, therefore, went and entered the place where Joseph was. And I was sitting at his feet looking at him, for the signs of death already appeared in his countenance. And that blessed old man raised his head, and kept his eyes fixed on my face; but he had no power of speaking to me, on account of the agonies of death, which held him in their grasp. But he kept fetching many sighs. And I held his hands for a whole hour; and he turned his face to me, and made signs for me not to leave him. Thereafter I put my hand upon his breast, and perceived his soul now near his throat, preparing to depart from its receptacle.

And when my virgin mother saw me touching

his body, she also touched his feet. And finding them already dead and destitute of heat, she said to me: "O my beloved son, assuredly his feet are already beginning to stiffen, and they are as cold as snow." Accordingly she summoned his sons and daughters, and said to them: "Come, as many as there are of you, and go to your father; for assuredly he is now at the very point of death." And Assia, his daughter, answered and said: "Woe's me, O my brothers, this is certainly the same disease that my beloved mother died of." And she lamented and shed tears; and all Joseph's other children mourned along with her. I also, and my mother Mary, wept along with them.

—*The History of Joseph the Carpenter*

As the all-holy glorious mother of God and ever-virgin Mary, as was her wont, was going to the holy tomb of our Lord to burn incense, and bending her holy knees, she was importunate that Christ our God who had been born of her should return to her. And the Jews, seeing her lingering by the divine sepulchre, came to the chief priests, saying: "Mary goes every day to the tomb." And the chief priests, having summoned the guards set by them not to allow any one to pray at the holy sepulchre, inquired about her, whether in truth it were so. And the guards answered and said that they had seen no such thing, God having not allowed them to see her when there. And on one of the days, it being the preparation, the holy Mary, as was her wont, came to the sepulchre; and while she was praying, it came to pass that the heavens were opened, and the archangel Gabriel came down to her and said: "Hail, thou that didst bring forth Christ our God! Thy prayer having come through to the heavens to Him who was born of thee, has been accepted; and from this time, according to thy request, thou having left the world, shall go to the heavenly places to thy Son, into the true and everlasting life."

And having heard this from the holy archangel, she returned to holy Bethlehem, having along with her three virgins who ministered unto her. And after having rested a short time, she sat up and said to the virgins: "Bring me a censer, that I may pray."

. . .

And while she was praying, I John came, the Holy Spirit having snatched me up by a cloud from Ephesus, and set me in the place where the mother of my Lord was lying. And having gone in beside her, and glorified Him who had been born of her, I said: "Hail, mother of my Lord, who didst bring forth Christ our God, rejoice that in great glory thou art going out of this life." And the holy mother of God glorified God, because I John had come to her, remembering the voice of the Lord, saying: "Behold thy mother, and, Behold thy son."

. . .

And there came a voice out of the heavens saying the Amen. And I John heard this voice; and the Holy Spirit said to me: "John, hast thou heard this voice that spoke in the heaven after the prayer was ended?" And I answered and said: "Yes, I heard." And the Holy Spirit said to me: "This voice which thou didst hear denotes that the appearance of thy brethren the apostles is at hand, and of the holy powers that they are coming hither to-day."

And at this I John prayed.

And the Holy Spirit said to the apostles: "Let all of you together, having come by the clouds from the ends of the world, be assembled to holy Bethlehem by a whirlwind, on account of the mother of our Lord Jesus Christ; Peter from Rome, Paul from Tiberia, Thomas from Hither India, James from Jerusalem." Andrew, Peter's brother, and Philip, Luke, and Simon the Cananaean, and Thaddaeus who had fallen asleep, were raised by the Holy Spirit out of their tombs; to whom the Holy Spirit said: "Do not think that it is now the resurrection; but on this account you have risen out of your tombs, that you may go to give greeting to the honor and wonder-working of the mother of our Lord and Savior Jesus Christ, because the day of her departure is at hand, of her going up into the heavens." And Mark likewise coming round, was present from Alexandria; he also with the rest, as has been said before, from each country. And Peter being lifted up by a cloud, stood between heaven and earth, the Holy Spirit keeping him steady. And at the same time, the rest of the apostles also, having been snatched up in clouds, were found along with Peter. And thus by the Holy Spirit, as has been said, they all came together.

And having gone in beside the mother of our Lord and God, and having adored, we said: "Fear not, nor grieve; God the Lord, who was born of thee, will take thee out of this world with glory." And rejoicing in God her Savior, she sat up in the bed, and said to the apostles: "Now have I believed that our Master and God is coming from heaven, and I shall behold Him, and thus depart from this life, as I have seen that you have come. And I wish you to tell me how you knew that I was departing and came to me, and from what countries and through what distance you have come hither, that you have thus made haste to visit me. For neither has He who was born of me, our Lord Jesus Christ, the God of the universe, concealed it; for I am persuaded even now that He is the Son of the Most High."

And Peter answered and said to the apostles: "Let us each, according to what the Holy Spirit announced and commanded us, give full information to the mother of our Lord." And I John answered and said: "Just as I was going in to the holy altar in Ephesus to perform divine service, the Holy Spirit says to me, 'The time of the departure of the mother of thy Lord is at hand; go to Bethlehem to salute her.' And a cloud of light snatched me up, and set me down in the door where thou art lying." Peter also answered: "And I, living in Rome, about dawn heard a voice through the Holy Spirit saying to me, 'The mother of thy Lord is to depart, as the time is at hand; go to Bethlehem to salute her.' And, behold, a cloud of light snatched me up; and I beheld also the other apostles coming to me on clouds, and a voice saying to me, 'Go all to Bethlehem.'" And Paul also answered and said: "And I, living in a city at no great distance from Rome, called the country of Tiberia, heard the Holy Spirit saying to me, 'The mother of thy Lord, having left this world, is making her course to the celestial regions through her departure; but go thou also to Bethlehem to salute her.' And, behold, a cloud of light having snatched me up, set me down in the same place as you." And Thomas also answered and said: "And I, traversing the country of the Indians, when the preaching was prevailing by the grace of Christ, and the king's sister's son Labdanus by name, was about to be sealed by me in the palace, on a sudden the Holy Spirit says to me, 'Do thou also, Thomas, go to Bethlehem to salute the mother of thy Lord, because she is taking her departure to the heavens.'

And a cloud of light having snatched me up, set me down beside you." And Mark also answered and said: "And when I was finishing the canon of the third day in the city of Alexandria, just as I was praying, the Holy Spirit snatched me up, and brought me to you." And James also answered and said: "While I was in Jerusalem, the Holy Spirit commanded me, saying, 'Go to Bethlehem, because the mother of thy Lord is taking her departure.' And, behold, a cloud of light having snatched me up, set me beside you." And Matthew also answered and said: "I have glorified and do glorify God, because when I was in a boat and overtaken by a storm, the sea raging with its waves, on a sudden a cloud of light overshadowing the stormy billow, changed it to a calm, and having snatched me up, set me down beside you." And those who had come before likewise answered, and gave an account of how they had come. And Bartholomew said: "I was in the Thebais proclaiming the word, and behold the Holy Spirit says to me, 'The mother of thy Lord is taking her departure; go, then, to salute her in Bethlehem.' And, behold, a cloud of light having snatched me up, brought me to you."

. . .

And while we were all praying, there appeared innumerable multitudes of angels, and the Lord mounted upon cherubim in great power; and, behold, a stream of light coming to the holy virgin, because of the presence of her only begotten Son, and all the powers of the heavens fell down and adored Him. And the Lord, speaking to His mother, said: "Mary." And she answered and said: "Here am I, Lord."

. . .

And then the face of the mother of the Lord shone brighter than the light, and she rose up and blessed each of the apostles with her own hand, and all gave glory to God; and the Lord stretched forth His undefiled hands, and received her holy and blameless soul. And with the departure of her blameless soul the place was filled with perfume and ineffable light; and, behold, a voice out of the heaven was heard, saying: "Blessed art thou among women."

—*The Book of John Concerning the Falling Asleep of Mary*

On the twentieth of the month Tobi, they were all gathered together at the altar, and Jesus appeared and greeted them. He bade Peter prepare the altar because "I must needs take a great offering from your midst on the morrow, before that each one of you goes to the lot that hath fallen to him to preach therein." He then ordained Peter archbishop, and others, including Evodius, presbyters and also deacons, readers, psalmists, and doorkeepers; and departed to heaven. They remained, wondering what the offering was to be.

On the twenty-first of Tobi Jesus returned, on the chariot of the cherubim, with thousands of angels, and David the sweet singer. We besought him to tell what the great offering was to be, and he told them it was his mother whom he was to take to himself.

We all wept, and Peter asked if it was not possible that Mary should never die, and then if she might not be left to them for a few days. But the Lord said that her time was accomplished.

The women, and also Mary, wept, but Jesus consoled her. She said: "I have heard that death has many terrible faces. How shall I bear to see them?" He said: "How dost thou fear his divine shape when the Life of all the world is with thee?" And he kissed her and blessed them all, and bade Peter look upon the altar for heavenly garments which the Lord had sent to shroud Mary in.

Mary arose and was arrayed in the garments, and turned to the east and uttered a prayer in the language of heaven, and then lay down, still facing eastward.

. . .

He comforted her and said to the apostles: "Let us withdraw outside for a little while, for Death cannot approach while I am here." And they went out and he sat on a stone, and looked up to heaven and groaned and said: "I have overcome thee, O Death, that dwellest in the store houses of the south. Come, appear to my virgin mother: but not in fearful shape." He appeared, and when she saw him, her soul leaped into the bosom of her son—white as snow, and he wrapped it in garments of fine linen and gave it to Michael.

. . .

They reentered the house and found her lying dead, and Jesus blessed her.

Jesus wrapped the body in the heavenly garments, and they were fastened thereto. He bade the apostles take up the body, Peter bearing the head and John the feet, and carry it to a new tomb in the field of Jehoshapat, and watch it for three and a half days.

. . .

Jesus ascended with Mary's soul in the chariot of the cherubim. At dawn on the sixteenth of Mesore, Jesus appeared. Peter said: "We are grieved we have not seen the mother since her death." Jesus said: "She shall now come." The chariot of the cherubim appeared with the Virgin seated in it. There were greetings. Jesus bade the apostles go and preach in all the world. He spent all that day with us and with his Mother, and gave us the salutation of peace and went up to heaven in glory.

—*The Assumption of the Virgin*

TWO

Jesus's Birth

"Utter not this mystery"

The baby Jesus lying in a manger, in a cave, surrounded by friendly and adoring animals, is a popular image on Christmas cards. But it is not a scene found in the Bible. The Nativity is only told in the opening chapters of two gospels—Matthew and Luke, neither of which mentions a cave, an ox, or an ass—and as early as the first century Christians were hungering for more details about the Nativity. Later scriptures provided them: Jesus was born in a cave in the Proto-Gospel of James, while the adoring ox and ass are found in the Gospel of Pseudo-Matthew.

One of the chief intentions of the writers of these accounts was to stress that Jesus was born of a virgin woman. A striking example of this is found in the Epistle of the Apostles, which was probably composed in the middle of the second century to refute Gnostic teachings. It takes the form of a postresurrection dialogue between Jesus and his disciples, a form popular with Gnostics. Yet the ideas that Jesus propounds are strictly orthodox, including that of the virgin birth. In a startling description of his own conception, Jesus claims that he himself appeared as the angel Gabriel before leaping into his mother's womb. The Questions of

Bartholomew, which may date from the third century, provides another dramatic account of the Annunciation. It has Mary telling the story, after the disciples have plucked up the courage to ask her how she conceived Jesus. In the Proto-Gospel of James, when word gets out that Mary is pregnant, she and Joseph are first scolded by a priest for their alleged wantonness, then made to drink a mystical lie-detecting liquid, to prove their protestations of chastity. This ritual is explained a little more clearly in the Gospel of Pseudo-Matthew.

Mary's perpetual virginity was first described in noncanonical accounts of Jesus's birth. This idea seems to have excited a good deal of skepticism in the early Church. Clement of Alexandria (A.D. 150–215) wrote in his book *The Stromata or Miscellanies* that most people believed Mary had ceased to be a virgin in the course of giving birth, but they are wrong: "for some say that, after she brought forth, she was found, when examined, to be a virgin." Perhaps he had in mind the Proto-Gospel of James; for here, after the birth of Jesus, Mary is examined by a skeptical midwife, who is amazed to discover that the new mother had indeed remained a virgin postpartum.

The writers of these accounts may have been encouraged to espouse Mary's virginity by the fact that the Bible has little to say on the subject. Only two of the gospels claim that Mary conceived as a virgin. It was important to writers of these texts to defend Jesus against allegations of illegitimacy. But they also wanted to reinforce the belief that he was God.

Other noncanonical signs of the divinity of Jesus lay in the supernatural events surrounding his birth: this was no blood-and-guts labor. Shortly before Jesus's birth in the Proto-Gospel of James, time suddenly stands still, as Joseph walks outside. When he reenters the cave, a miraculously bright light obscures Mary's labor, until Jesus "appears." In the Arabic Infancy Gospel, the cave where Jesus is born is also filled with a blinding light.

Such accounts tread dangerously close to the heresy of docetism, a belief that Jesus's physical body was an illusion, which was common in the early Church. Gnostic texts that mention Jesus's birth, however, are clearly docetic. In the third-century Second Treatise of the Great Seth, Jesus describes himself as a spiritual being taking a human form.

The Gospel of Philip, which was discovered at Nag Hammadi and dates from the late second or early third century, dismisses the notion of the virgin birth. This text draws a distinction between those who understand Jesus's true message and those who do not. People who look for outward signs, it suggests, have missed the point.

NOW there was a council of the priests, and they said: "Let us make a veil for the temple of the Lord." And the priest said: "Call unto me pure virgins of the tribe of David." And the officers departed and sought and found seven virgins. And the priests called to mind the child Mary, that she was of the tribe of David and was undefiled before God: and the officers went and fetched her. And they brought them into the temple of the Lord, and the priest said: "Cast me lots, which of you shall weave the gold and the undefiled and the fine linen and the silk and the hyacinthine, and the scarlet and the true purple." And the lot of the true purple and the scarlet fell unto Mary, and she took them and went unto her house.

. . .

And she took the pitcher and went forth to fill it with water: and lo a voice saying: "Hail, thou that art highly favored; the Lord is with thee: blessed art thou among women."

And she looked about her upon the right hand and upon the left, to see whence this voice should be: and being filled with trembling she went to her house and set down the pitcher, and took the purple and sat down upon her seat and drew out the thread.

And behold an angel of the Lord stood before her saying: "Fear not, Mary, for thou hast found grace before the Lord of all things, and thou shalt conceive of his word." And she, when she heard it, questioned in herself, saying: "Shall I verily conceive of the living God, and bring forth after the manner of all women?" And the angel of the Lord said: "Not so, Mary, for a power of the Lord shall overshadow thee: wherefore also that holy thing which shall be born of thee shall be called the Son of the Highest. And thou shalt call his name Jesus: for he shall save his people from their sins." And Mary said: "Behold the handmaid of the Lord is before him: be it unto me according to thy word."

—*The Proto-Gospel of James*

For ye know that the angel Gabriel brought the message unto Mary. And we answered: "Yea, Lord." He answered and said unto us: "Remember ye not, then, that I said unto you a little while ago: I became an angel among the angels, and I became all things in all?" We said unto him: "Yea, Lord." Then answered he and said unto us: "On that day whereon I took the form of the angel Gabriel, I appeared unto Mary and spake with her. Her heart accepted me, and she believed, and I formed myself and entered into her body. I became flesh, for I alone was a minister unto myself in that which concerned Mary in the appearance of the shape of an angel. For so must I needs do. Thereafter did I return to my Father."

—*The Epistle of the Apostles*

Now the apostles were in the place with Mary. And Bartholomew came and said unto Peter and

Andrew and John: "Let us ask her that is highly favored how she conceived the incomprehensible, or how she bore him that cannot be carried, or how she brought forth so much greatness." But they doubted to ask her. Bartholomew therefore said unto Peter: "Thou that art the chief, and my teacher, draw near and ask her." But Peter said to John: "Thou art a virgin and undefiled [and beloved] and thou must ask her."

And as they all doubted and disputed, Bartholomew came near unto her with a cheerful countenance and said to her: "Thou that art highly favored, the tabernacle of the Most High, unblemished, we, even all the apostles, ask thee to tell us how thou didst conceive the incomprehensible, or how thou didst bear him that cannot be carried, or how thou didst bring forth so much greatness."

But Mary said unto them: "Ask me not concerning this mystery. If I should begin to tell you, fire will issue forth out of my mouth and consume all the world." But they continued yet the more to ask her. And she, for she could not refuse to hear the apostles, said: "Let us stand up in prayer."

. . .

And when she had ended the prayer she began to say unto them: "Let us sit down upon the ground; and come thou, Peter the chief, and sit on my right hand and put thy left hand beneath mine armpit; and thou, Andrew, do so on my left hand;

and thou, John, the virgin, hold together my bosom; and thou, Bartholomew, set thy knees against my back and hold my shoulders, lest when I begin to speak my bones be loosed one from another."

And when they had so done she began to say: "When I abode in the temple of God and received my food from an angel, on a certain day there appeared unto me one in the likeness of an angel, but his face was incomprehensible, and he had not in his hand bread or a cup, as did the angel which came to me aforetime.

"And straightway the robe [veil] of the temple was rent and there was a very great earthquake, and I fell upon the earth, for I was not able to endure the sight of him. But he put his hand beneath me and raised me up, and I looked up into heaven and there came a cloud of dew and sprinkled me from the head to the feet, and he wiped me with his robe. And said unto me: 'Hail, thou that art highly favored, the chosen vessel, grace inexhaustible.' And he smote his garment upon the right hand and there came a very great loaf, and he set it upon the altar of the temple and did eat of it first himself, and gave unto me also. And again he smote his garment upon the left hand and there came a very great cup full of wine: and he set it upon the altar of the temple and did drink of it first himself, and gave also unto me. And I beheld and saw the bread and the cup whole as they were.

And he said unto me: 'Yet three years, and I will send my word unto thee and thee shall conceive my son, and through him shall the whole creation be saved. Peace be unto thee, my beloved, and my peace shall be with thee continually.' And when he had so said he vanished away from mine eyes, and the temple was restored as it had been before."

And as she was saying this, fire issued out of her mouth; and the world was at the point to come to an end: but Jesus appeared quickly and said unto Mary: "Utter not this mystery, or this day my whole creation will come to an end." And the apostles were taken with fear lest haply the Lord should be wroth with them.

—*The Questions of Bartholomew*

And Mary rejoiced and went away unto Elizabeth her kinswoman: and she knocked at the door. And Elizabeth when she heard it cast down the scarlet and ran to the door and opened it, and when she saw Mary she blessed her and said: "Whence is this to me that the mother of my Lord should come unto me? For behold that which is in me leaped and blessed thee." And Mary forgat the mysteries which Gabriel the archangel had told her, and she looked up unto the heaven and said: "Who am I, Lord, that all the generations of the earth do bless me?" And she abode three months with Elizabeth, and day by day her womb grew: and Mary was afraid and departed unto her house and hid herself from the children of Israel. Now she was sixteen years old when these mysteries came to pass.

Now it was the sixth month with her, and behold Joseph came from his building, and he entered into his house and found her great with child. And he smote his face, and cast himself down upon the ground on sackcloth and wept bitterly, saying: "With what countenance shall I look unto the Lord my God? And what prayer shall I make concerning this maiden? For I received her out of the temple of the Lord my God a virgin, and have not kept her safe. Who is he that hath ensnared me? Who hath done this evil in mine house and hath defiled the virgin? Is not the story of Adam repeated in me? For as at the hour of his giving thanks the serpent came and found Eve alone and deceived her, so hath it befallen me also." And Joseph arose from off the sackcloth and called Mary and said unto her: "O thou that wast cared for by God, why hast thou done this? Thou hast forgotten the Lord thy God. Why hast thou humbled thy soul, thou that wast nourished up in the Holy of Holies and didst receive food at the hand of an angel?" But she wept bitterly, saying: "I am pure and I know not a man." And Joseph said unto her: "Whence then is that which is in thy womb?" And she said: "As the Lord my God liveth, I know not whence it is come unto me."

And Joseph was sore afraid and ceased from speaking unto her, and pondered what he should do with her. And Joseph said: "If I hide her sin, I shall be found fighting against the law of the Lord: and if I manifest her unto the children of Israel, I fear lest that which is in her be the seed of an angel, and I shall be found delivering up innocent blood to the judgment of death. What then shall I do? I will let her go from me privily." And the night came upon him. And behold an angel of the Lord appeared unto him in a dream, saying: "Fear not this child, for that which is in her is of the Holy Ghost, and she shall bear a son and thou shall call his name Jesus, for he shall save his people from their sins." And Joseph arose from sleep and glorified the God of Israel which had shown this favor unto her: and he watched over her.

Now Annas the scribe came unto him and said to him: "Wherefore didst thou not appear in our assembly?" And Joseph said unto him: "I was weary with the journey, and I rested the first day." And Annas turned him about and saw Mary great with child. And he went hastily to the priest and said unto him: "Joseph, to whom thou bearest witness, hath sinned grievously." And the priest said: "Wherein?" And he said: "The virgin whom he received out of the temple of the Lord, he hath defiled her, and married her by stealth, and hath not declared it to the children of Israel." And the priest answered and said: "Hath Joseph done this?" And Annas the scribe said: "Send officers, and thou shalt find the virgin great with child." And the officers went and found as he had said, and they brought her together with Joseph unto the place of judgment. And the priest said: "Mary, wherefore hast thou done this, and wherefore hast thou humbled thy soul and forgotten the Lord thy God, thou that wast nurtured in the Holy of Holies and didst receive food at the hand of an angel and didst hear the hymns and didst dance before the Lord, wherefore hast thou done this?"

But she wept bitterly, saying: "As the Lord my God liveth I am pure before him and I know not a man." And the priest said unto Joseph: "Wherefore hast thou done this?" And Joseph said: "As the Lord my God liveth I am pure as concerning her." And the priest said: "Bear no false witness but speak the truth: thou hast married her by stealth and hast not declared it unto the children of Israel, and hast not bowed thine head under the mighty hand that thy seed should be blessed." And Joseph held his peace.

And the priest said: "Restore the virgin whom thou didst receive out of the temple of the Lord." And Joseph was full of weeping. And the priest said: "I will give you to drink of the water of the conviction of the Lord, and it will make manifest your sins before your eyes." And the priest took thereof and made Joseph drink and sent him into the hill-country. And he returned whole. He made Mary also drink and sent her into the hill-country. And she returned whole. And all the people marveled, because sin appeared not in them. And the priest said: "If the Lord God hath not made your sin manifest, neither do I condemn you." And he let them go. And Joseph took Mary and departed unto his house rejoicing, and glorifying the God of Israel.

—*The Proto-Gospel of James*

And when any one that had lied drank this water, and walked seven times round the altar, God used to show some sign in his face. When, therefore, Joseph had drunk in safety, and had walked round the altar seven times, no sign of sin appeared in him. Then all the priests, and the officers, and the people justified him, saying: "Blessed art thou, seeing that no charge has been found good against thee." And they summoned Mary, and said: "And what excuse canst thou have? Or what greater sign can appear in thee than the conception of thy womb, which betrays thee? This only we require of thee, that since Joseph is pure regarding thee, thou confess who it is that has beguiled thee. For it is better that thy confession should betray thee, than that the wrath of God should set a mark on thy face, and expose thee in the midst of the people."

Then Mary said, steadfastly and without trembling: "O Lord God, King over all, who knowest all secrets, if there be any pollution in me, or any sin, or any evil desires, or unchastity, expose me in the sight of all the people, and make me an example of punishment to all." Thus saying, she went up to the altar of the Lord boldly, and drank the water of drinking, and walked round the altar seven times, and no spot was found in her.

—*The Gospel of Pseudo-Matthew*

Now there went out a decree from Augustus the king that all that were in Bethlehem of Judaea should be recorded. And Joseph said: "I will record my sons: but this child, what shall I do with her? How shall I record her? As my wife? Nay, I am ashamed. Or as my daughter? But all the children of Israel know that she is not my daughter. This day of the Lord shall do as the Lord willeth." And he saddled the she-ass, and set her upon it, and his son led it and Joseph followed after. And they drew near (unto Bethlehem) within three miles: and Joseph turned himself about and saw her of a sad countenance and said within himself: "Peradventure that which is within her paineth her." And again Joseph turned himself about and saw her laughing, and said unto her: "Mary, what aileth thee that I see thy face at one time laughing and at another time sad?" And Mary said unto Joseph: "It is because I behold two people with mine eyes, the one weeping and lamenting and the other rejoicing and exulting."

And they came to the midst of the way, and Mary said unto him: "Take me down from the ass, for that which is within me presseth me, to come forth." And he took her down from the ass and said unto her: "Whither shall I take thee to hide thy shame? For the place is desert."

And he found a cave there and brought her into it, and set his sons by her: and he went forth and sought for a midwife of the Hebrews in the country of Bethlehem.

Now I Joseph was walking, and I walked not. And I looked up to the air and saw the air in amazement. And I looked up unto the pole of the heaven and saw it standing still, and the fowls of the heaven without motion. And I looked upon the earth and saw a dish set, and workmen lying by it, and their hands were in the dish: and they that were chewing chewed not, and they that were lifting the food lifted it not, and they that put it to their mouth put it not thereto, but the faces of all of them were looking upward. And behold there were sheep being driven, and they went not forward but stood still; and the shepherd lifted his hand to smite them with his staff, and his hand remained up. And I looked upon the stream of the river and saw the mouths of the kids upon the water and they drank not. And of a sudden all things moved onward in their course.

And behold a woman coming down from the hill-country, and she said to me: "Man, whither goest thou?" And I said: "I seek a midwife of the Hebrews." And she answered and said unto me: "Art thou of Israel?" And I said unto her: "Yea." And she said: "And who is she that bringeth forth in the cave?" And I said: "She that is betrothed unto me." And she said to me: "Is she not thy wife?" And I said to her: "It is Mary that was nurtured up in the temple of the Lord: and I received her to wife by lot: and she is not my wife, but she hath conception by the Holy Ghost."

And the midwife said unto him: "Is this the truth?" And Joseph said unto her: "Come hither and see." And the midwife went with him.

And they stood in the place of the cave: and behold a bright cloud overshadowing the cave. And the midwife said: "My soul is magnified this day, because mine eyes have seen marvelous things: for salvation is born unto Israel." And immediately the cloud withdrew itself out of the cave, and a great light appeared in the cave so that our eyes could not endure it. And little by little that light withdrew itself until the young child appeared: and it went and took the breast of its mother Mary.

And the midwife cried aloud and said: "Great

unto me today is this day, in that I have seen this new sight." And the midwife went forth of the cave and Salome met her. And she said to her: "Salome, Salome, a new sight have I to tell thee. A virgin hath brought forth, which her nature alloweth not." And Salome said: "As the Lord my God liveth, if I make not trial and prove her nature I will not believe that a virgin hath brought forth."

And the midwife went in and said unto Mary: "Order thyself, for there is no small contention arisen concerning thee." And Salome made trial and cried out and said: "Woe unto mine iniquity and mine unbelief, because I have tempted the living God, and lo, my hand falleth away from me in fire." And she bowed her knees unto the Lord, saying: "O God of my fathers, remember that I am the seed of Abraham and Isaac and Jacob: make me not a public example unto the children of Israel, but restore me unto the poor, for thou knowest, Lord, that in thy name did I perform my cures, and did receive my hire of thee."

—*The Proto-Gospel of James*

Wherefore, after sunset, the old woman, and Joseph with her, came to the cave, and they both went in. And, behold, it was filled with lights more beautiful than the gleaming of lamps and candles, and more splendid than the light of the sun. The child, enwrapped in swaddling clothes, was sucking the breast of the Lady Mary His mother, being placed in a stall. And when both were wondering at this light, the old woman asked the Lady Mary: "Art thou the mother of this child?" And when the Lady Mary gave her assent, she said: "Thou art not at all like the daughters of Eve." The Lady Mary said: "As my son has no equal among children, so his mother has no equal among women." The old woman replied: "My mistress, I came to get payment; I have been for a long time affected with palsy." Our mistress the Lady Mary said to her: "Place thy hands upon the child." And the old woman did so, and was immediately cured. Then she went forth, saying: "Henceforth I will be the attendant and servant of this child all the days of my life."

. . .

And it came to pass, when the Lord Jesus was born at Bethlehem of Judaea, in the time of King Herod, behold, magi came from the east to Jerusalem, as Zeraduscht had predicted; and there were with them gifts, gold, and frankincense, and myrrh. And they adored Him, and presented to Him their gifts. Then the Lady Mary took one of the swaddling-bands, and, on account of the smallness of her means, gave it to them; and they received it from her with the greatest marks of honor. And in the same hour there appeared to them an angel in the form of that star which had before guided them on their journey; and they went away, following the guidance of its light, until they arrived in their own country.

And their kings and chief men came together to them, asking what they had seen or done, how they had gone and come back, what they had brought with them. And they showed them that swathing-cloth which the Lady Mary had given them. Wherefore they celebrated a feast, and, according to their custom, lighted a fire and worshipped it, and threw that swathing-cloth into it; and the fire laid hold of it, and enveloped it. And when the fire had gone out, they took out the swathing-cloth exactly as it had been before, just as if the fire had not touched it. Wherefore they began to kiss it, and to put it on their heads and their eyes, saying: "This verily is the truth without doubt. Assuredly it is a great thing that the fire was not able to burn or destroy it." Then they took it, and with the greatest honor laid it up among their treasures.

—*The Arabic Infancy Gospel*

And on the third day after the birth of our Lord Jesus Christ, the most blessed Mary went forth out of the cave, and entering a stable, placed the child in the stall, and the ox and the ass adored Him. Then was fulfilled that which was said by Isaiah the prophet, saying: "The ox knoweth his owner, and the ass his master's crib. The very animals, therefore, the ox and the ass, having Him in their midst, incessantly adored Him." Then was fulfilled that which was said by Abacuc the prophet, saying: "Between two animals thou art made manifest." In the same place Joseph remained with Mary three days.

—*The Gospel of Pseudo-Matthew*

I visited a bodily dwelling. I cast out the one who was in it first, and I went in. And the whole multitude of the archons became troubled. And all the matter of the archons, as well as all the begotten powers of the earth, was shaken when it saw the likeness of the Image, since it was mixed. And I am the one who was in it, not resembling him who was in it first. For he was an earthly man, but I, I am from above the heavens. I did not refuse them even to become a Christ, but I did not reveal myself to them in the love which was coming forth from me. I revealed that I am a stranger to the regions below.

—*The Second Treatise of the Great Seth*

Some say, "Mary conceived by the Holy Spirit." They do not know what they are saying. When did a woman ever conceive by a woman?

—*The Gospel of Philip*

THREE

Jesus's Childhood

"Who will he be?"

The Bible says almost nothing about Jesus between the time of his birth and the beginning of his ministry, a span of roughly thirty years. Jesus's childhood is mentioned only once in the Bible: the Gospel of Luke describes Mary and Joseph finding him teaching in the temple when he is twelve years old. For apocrypha writers, this left a tantalizing gap. The infancy gospels, as the books that deal with Jesus's childhood are known, are filled with detailed, often outlandish stories of Jesus from a toddler to his early adolescence.

The tales of Jesus's early childhood are set in Egypt, where the family has escaped from the murderous wrath of Herod. At the age of two or three, according to the Gospel of Pseudo-Matthew, Jesus is taming dragons and inspiring the adoration of lions, which guide him and his terrified parents through the desert. In the Arabic Infancy Gospel, Jesus meets Judas, the apostle who was later to betray him, as a child, and drives Satan out of him. The family also encounters two robbers, who Jesus prophesies will be crucified beside him in thirty years' time—further scaring his mother. But in this gospel, Mary is a formidable woman: when people are cured with water that has been used to wash Baby Jesus,

Mary is the one they speak to, and she organizes a number of miraculous healings.

The noncanonical accounts of Jesus's childhood were probably written for Christians who had read the canonical gospels and wondered what Jesus was like as a child. And so they show that just as he was as a man, the child Jesus was aware that he was sent from God and had supernatural powers—and not only supernatural gifts, but power over life and death.

In the Infancy Gospel of Thomas, these powers are taken to quite alarming levels. The gospel, which is thought to be one of the earliest such texts, referred to by Irenaeus, Bishop of Lyon, in the second century, portrays Jesus as a supernatural brat. He cripples, blinds, and kills people who irritate him, cruelly ridicules three teachers, and is entirely beyond the control of his parents. At one point, Joseph begs Mary to keep Jesus at home, to stop him killing those who vex him. This portrayal of an omnipotent, strong-willed child may have been influenced by pagan myths: in classical antiquity, heroes' actions were often foreseen in their childhoods. But as Jesus grows older he learns to use his powers more compassionately, and the gospel ends on a recognizably Christian note.

For the writer of the Arabic Infancy Gospel, Luke's cursory description of the boy Jesus in the temple was an opportunity to exploit. He describes Jesus astounding his elders there with his knowledge of "physics and metaphysics, hyperphysics and hypophysics . . . and other things beyond the reach of any created intellect." Another story about Jesus's childhood is in the Pistis Sophia (Faith Wisdom), a Gnostic work, written in the form of a dialogue between Jesus and his disciples. This third- or fourth-century text surfaced in 1773, when it was sold to an English manuscript collector, and was published eight years later.

AND having come to a certain cave, and wishing to rest in it, the blessed Mary dismounted from her beast, and sat down with the child Jesus in her bosom. And there were with Joseph three boys, and with Mary a girl, going on the journey along with them. And, lo, suddenly there came forth from the cave many dragons; and when the children saw them, they cried out in great terror. Then Jesus went down from the bosom of His mother, and stood on His feet before the dragons; and they adored Jesus, and thereafter retired. Then was fulfilled that which was said by David the prophet, saying: "Praise the Lord from the earth, ye dragons; ye dragons, and all ye deeps." And the young child Jesus, walking before them, commanded them to hurt no man. But Mary and Joseph were very much afraid lest the child should be hurt by the dragons. And Jesus said to them: "Do not be afraid, and do not consider me to be a little child; for I am and always have been perfect; and all the beasts of the forest must needs be tame before me."

Lions and panthers adored Him likewise, and accompanied him in the desert. Wherever Joseph and the blessed Mary went, they went before them showing them the way, and bowing their heads; and showing their submission by wagging their tails, they adored Him with great reverence. Now at first, when Mary saw the lions and the panthers, and various kinds of wild beasts, coming about them, she was very much afraid. But the infant Jesus looked into her face with a joyful countenance, and said: "Be not afraid, mother; for they come not to do thee harm, but they make haste to serve both thee and me." With these words He drove all fear from her heart. And the lions kept walking with them, and with the oxen, and the asses, and the beasts of burden which carried their baggage, and did not hurt a single one of them, though they kept beside them; but they were tame among the sheep and the rams which they had brought with them from Judaea, and which they had with them. They walked among wolves, and feared nothing; and no one of them was hurt by another. Then was fulfilled that which was spoken by the prophet: Wolves shall feed with lambs; the lion and the ox shall eat straw together. There were together two oxen drawing a wagon with provision for the journey, and the lions directed them in their path.

And it came to pass on the third day of their journey, while they were walking, that the blessed Mary was fatigued by the excessive heat of the sun in the desert; and seeing a palm tree, she said to Joseph: "Let me rest a little under the shade of this tree." Joseph therefore made haste, and led her to the palm, and made her come down from her beast. And as the blessed Mary was sitting there, she looked up to the foliage of the palm, and saw it full of fruit, and said to Joseph: "I wish it were possible to get some of the fruit of this palm." And Joseph said to her: "I wonder that thou sayest this, when thou seest how high the palm tree is; and that thou thinkest of eating of its fruit. I am thinking more of the want of water, because the skins are now empty, and we have none wherewith to refresh ourselves and our cattle." Then the child Jesus, with a joyful countenance, reposing in the bosom of His mother, said to the palm: "O tree, bend thy branches, and refresh my mother with thy fruit." And immediately at these words the palm bent its top down to the very feet of the blessed Mary; and they gathered from it fruit, with which they were all refreshed. And after they had gathered all its fruit, it remained bent down, waiting the order to rise from Him who had commanded it to stoop. Then Jesus said to it: "Raise thyself, O palm tree, and be strong, and be the companion of my trees, which are in the paradise of my Father; and open from thy roots a vein of water which has been hid in the earth, and let the waters flow, so that we may be satisfied from thee." And it rose up immediately, and at its root there began to come forth a spring of water exceedingly clear and cool and sparkling. And when they saw the spring of water, they rejoiced with great joy, and were satisfied, themselves and all their cattle and their beasts. Wherefore they gave thanks to God.

And on the day after, when they were setting out thence, and in the hour in which they began their journey, Jesus turned to the palm, and said: "This privilege I give thee, O palm tree, that one of thy branches be carried away by my angels, and planted in the paradise of my Father. And this blessing I will confer upon thee, that it shall be said of all who conquer in any contest, 'You have attained the palm of victory.'" And while He was thus speaking, behold, an angel of the Lord appeared, and stood upon the palm tree; and taking off one of its branches, flew to heaven with the branch in his hand. And when they saw this, they fell on their faces, and became as it were dead. And Jesus said to them: "Why are your hearts possessed with fear? Do you not know that this palm, which I have caused to be transferred to paradise, shall be prepared for all the saints in the place of delights, as it has been prepared for us in this place of the wilderness?" And they were filled with joy; and being strengthened, they all rose up.

After this, while they were going on their journey, Joseph said to Jesus: "Lord, it is a boiling heat; if it please Thee, let us go by the sea-shore, that we may be able to rest in the cities on the coast." Jesus said to him: "Fear not, Joseph; I will shorten the way for you, so that what you would have taken thirty days to go over, you shall accomplish in this one day." And while they were thus speaking, behold, they looked forward, and began to see the mountains and cities of Egypt. And rejoicing and exulting, they came into the regions of Hermopolis, and entered into a certain city of Egypt which is called Sotinen; and because they knew no one there from whom they could ask hospitality, they went into a temple which was called the Capitol of Egypt. And in this temple there had been set up 355 idols, to each of which on its own day divine honors and sacred rites were paid. For the Egyptians belonging to the same city entered the Capitol, in which the priests told them how many sacrifices were offered each day, according to the honor in which the god was held.

And it came to pass, when the most blessed Mary went into the temple with the little child, that all the idols prostrated themselves on the ground, so that all of them were lying on their faces shattered and broken to pieces; and thus they plainly showed that they were nothing. Then was fulfilled that which was said by the prophet Isaiah: "Behold, the Lord will come upon a swift cloud, and will enter Egypt, and all the handiwork of the Egyptians shall be moved at His presence."

Then Affrodosius, the governor of that city, when news of this was brought to him, went to the temple with all his army. And the priests of the temple, when they saw Affrodosius with all his army coming into the temple, thought that he was making haste only to see vengeance taken on those on whose account the gods had fallen down. But when he came into the temple, and saw all the gods lying prostrate on their faces, he went up to the blessed Mary, who was carrying the Lord in her bosom, and adored Him, and said to all his army and all his friends: "Unless this were the God of our gods, our gods would not have fallen on their faces before Him; nor would they be lying prostrate in His presence: wherefore they silently confess that He is their Lord. Unless we, therefore, take care to do what we have seen our gods doing, we may run the risk of His anger, and all come to destruction, even as it happened to Pharaoh king of the Egyptians, who, not believing in powers so mighty, was drowned in the sea, with all his army." Then all the people of that same city believed in the Lord God through Jesus Christ.

—*The Gospel of Pseudo-Matthew*

And turning away from this place, they came to a desert; and hearing that it was infested by robbers, Joseph and the Lady Mary resolved to cross this region by night. But as they go along, behold, they see two robbers lying in the way, and along with them a great number of robbers, who were their associates, sleeping. Now those two robbers, into whose hands they had fallen, were Titus and Dumachus. Titus therefore said to Dumachus: "I beseech thee to let these persons go freely, and so that our comrades may not see them." And as Dumachus refused, Titus said to him again: "Take to thyself forty drachmas from me, and hold this as a pledge." At the same time he held out to him the belt which he had about his waist, to keep him from opening his mouth or speaking. And the Lady Mary, seeing that the robber had done them a kindness, said to him: "The Lord God will sustain thee by His right hand, and will grant thee remission of thy sins." And the Lord Jesus answered, and said to His mother: "Thirty years hence, O my mother, the Jews will crucify me at Jerusalem, and these two robbers will be raised upon the cross along with me, Titus on my right hand and Dumachus on my left; and after that day Titus shall go before me into Paradise." And she said: "God keep this from thee, my son." And they went thence toward a city of idols, which, as they came near it, was changed into sand-hills.

Hence they turned aside to that sycamore which is now called Matarea, and the Lord Jesus brought forth in Matarea a fountain in which the Lady Mary washed His shirt. And from the sweat of the Lord Jesus which she sprinkled there, balsam was produced in that region.

Thence they came down to Memphis, and saw Pharaoh, and remained three years in Egypt; and the Lord Jesus did in Egypt very many miracles which are recorded neither in the Gospel of the Infancy nor in the perfect Gospel.

And at the end of the three years He came back out of Egypt, and returned. And when they had arrived at Judaea, Joseph was afraid to enter it; but hearing that Herod was dead, and that Archelaus his son had succeeded him, he was afraid indeed, but he went into Judaea. And an angel of the Lord appeared to him, and said: "O Joseph, go into the city of Nazareth, and there abide."

Wonderful indeed, that the Lord of the world should be thus borne and carried about through the world!

. . .

Thereafter, going into the city of Bethlehem, they saw there many and grievous diseases infesting the eyes of the children, who were dying in consequence. And a woman was there with a sick son, whom, now very near death, she brought to the Lady Mary, who saw him as she was washing Jesus Christ. Then said the woman to her: "O my Lady Mary, look upon this son of mine, who is laboring under a grievous disease." And the Lady Mary listened to her, and said: "Take a little of that water in which I have washed my son, and sprinkle him with it." She therefore took a little of the water, as the Lady Mary had told her, and sprinkled it over her son. And when this was done his illness abated; and after sleeping a little, he rose up from sleep safe and sound. His mother rejoicing at this, again took him to the Lady Mary. And she said to her: "Give thanks to God, because He hath healed this thy son."

. . .

Another woman was living in the same place, whose son was tormented by Satan. He, Judas by name, as often as Satan seized him, used to bite all who came near him; and if he found no one near him, he used to bite his own hands and other limbs. The mother of this wretched creature, then, hearing the fame of the Lady Mary and her son Jesus, rose up and brought her son Judas with her to the Lady Mary. In the meantime, James and Joses had taken the child the Lord Jesus with them to play with the other children; and they had gone out of the house and sat down, and the Lord Jesus with them. And the demoniac Judas came up, and sat down at Jesus's right hand: then, being attacked by Satan in the same manner as usual, he wished to bite the Lord Jesus, but was not able; nevertheless he struck Jesus on the right side, whereupon He began to weep. And immediately Satan went forth out of that boy, fleeing like a mad dog. And this boy who struck Jesus, and out of whom Satan went forth in the shape of a dog, was Judas Iscariot, who betrayed Him to the Jews; and that same side on which Judas struck Him, the Jews transfixed with a lance.

. . .

On a certain day the Lord Jesus, running about and playing with the boys, passed the shop of a dyer, whose name was Salem; and he had in his shop many pieces of cloth which he was to dye. The Lord Jesus then, going into his shop, took up all the pieces of cloth, and threw them into a tub full of indigo. And when Salem came and saw his cloths destroyed, he began to cry out with a loud voice, and to reproach Jesus, saying: "Why hast thou done this to me, O son of Mary? Thou hast disgraced me before all my townsmen: for, seeing that everyone wished the color that suited himself, thou indeed hast come and destroyed them all." The Lord Jesus answered: "I shall change for thee the color of any piece of cloth which thou shalt wish to be changed." And immediately He began to take the pieces of cloth out of the tub, each of them of that color which the dyer wished, until He had taken them all out.

When the Jews saw this miracle and prodigy, they praised God.

And Joseph used to go about through the whole city, and take the Lord Jesus with him, when people sent for him in the way of his trade to make for them doors, and milk-pails, and beds, and chests; and the Lord Jesus was with him wherever he went. As often, therefore, as Joseph had to make anything a cubit or a span longer or shorter, wider or narrower, the Lord Jesus stretched His hand toward it; and as soon as He did so, it became such as Joseph wished.

—*The Arabic Infancy Gospel*

This little child Jesus when he was five years old was playing at the ford of a brook: and he gathered together the waters that flowed there into pools, and made them straightway clean, and commanded them by his word alone. And having made soft clay, he fashioned thereof twelve sparrows. And it was the Sabbath when he did these things. And there were also many other little children playing with him.

And a certain Jew when he saw what Jesus did, playing upon the Sabbath day, departed straightway and told his father Joseph: "Lo, thy child is at the brook, and he hath taken clay and fashioned twelve little birds, and hath polluted the Sabbath day." And Joseph came to the place and saw, and cried out to him, saying: "Wherefore doest thou these things on the Sabbath, which it is not lawful to do?" But Jesus clapped his hands together and cried out to the sparrows and said to them: "Go!" and the sparrows took their flight and went away chirping. And when the Jews saw it they were amazed, and departed and told their chief men that which they had seen Jesus do.

But the son of Annas the scribe was standing there with Joseph; and he took a branch of a willow and dispersed the waters which Jesus had gathered together. And when Jesus saw what was done, he was wroth and said unto him: "O evil, ungodly, and foolish one, what hurt did the pools and the waters do thee? Behold, now also thou shalt be withered like a tree, and shalt not bear leaves, neither root, nor fruit." And straightway that lad withered up wholly, but Jesus departed and went unto Joseph's house. But the parents of him that was withered took him up, bewailing his youth, and brought him to Joseph, and accused him: "for that thou hast such a child which doeth such deeds."

After that again he went through the village, and a child ran and dashed against his shoulder. And Jesus was provoked and said unto him: "Thou shalt not finish thy course." And immediately he fell down and died. But certain when they saw what was done said: "Whence was this young child born, for that every word of his is an accomplished work?" And the parents of him that was dead came unto Joseph, and blamed him, saying: "Thou that hast such a child canst not dwell with us in the village: or do thou teach him to bless and not to curse: for he slayeth our children."

And Joseph called the young child apart and admonished him, saying: "Wherefore doest thou such things, that these suffer and hate us and persecute us?" But Jesus said: "I know that these thy words are not thine: nevertheless for thy sake I will hold my peace: but they shall bear their punishment." And straightway they that accused him were smitten with blindness. And they that saw it were sore afraid and perplexed, and said concerning him that every word which he spake whether it were good or bad, was a deed, and became a marvel. And when they saw that Jesus had so done, Joseph arose and took hold upon his ear and wrung it sore. And the young child was wroth and said unto him: "It sufficeth thee to seek and not to find, and verily thou hast done unwisely: knowest thou not that I am thine? Vex me not."

Now a certain teacher, Zacchaeus by name, stood there and he heard in part when Jesus said these things to his father and he marveled greatly that being a young child he spake such matters. And after a few days he came near unto Joseph and said unto him: "Thou hast a wise child, and he hath understanding. Come, deliver him to me that he may learn letters. And I will teach him with the letters all knowledge and that he salute all the elders and honor them as grandfathers and fathers, and love them of his own years." And he told him all the letters from Alpha even to Omega clearly, with much questioning. But Jesus looked upon Zacchaeus the teacher and saith unto him: "Thou that knowest not the Alpha according to its nature, how canst thou teach others the Beta? Thou hypocrite, first, if thou knowest it, teach the Alpha, and then will we believe thee concerning the Beta." Then began he to confound the mouth of the teacher concerning the first letter, and he could not prevail to answer him. And in the hearing of many, the young child saith to Zacchaeus: "Hear, O teacher, the ordinance of the first letter and pay heed to this, how that it hath lines, and a middle mark, which thou seest, common to both, going apart; coming together, raised up on high, dancing, of three signs, like in kind: thou hast the rules of the Alpha."

Now when Zacchaeus the teacher heard such and so many allegories of the first letter spoken by the young child, he was perplexed at his answer and his instruction being so great, and said to them that were there: "Woe is me, wretch that I am, I am confounded: I have brought shame to myself by drawing to me this young child. Take him away, therefore I beseech thee, my brother Joseph: I cannot endure the severity of his look, I cannot once make clear my word. This young child is not earthly born: this is one that can tame even fire: be like this is one begotten before the making of the world. What belly bare this, what womb nurtured it? I know not. Woe is me, O my friend, he putteth me from my sense, I cannot follow his understanding. I have deceived myself, thrice wretched man that I am: I strove to get me a disciple and I am found to have a master. I think, O my friends, upon my shame, for that being old I have been overcome by a young child—and I am even ready to faint and to die because of the boy, for I am not able at this present hour to look him in the face. And when all men say that I have been overcome by a little child, what have I to say? and what can I tell concerning the lines of the first letter whereof he spake to me? I am ignorant, O my friends, for neither beginning nor end of it [or him] do I know. Wherefore I beseech thee, my brother Joseph, take him away unto thine house: for he is somewhat great, whether god or angel or what I should call him, I know not."

And as the Jews were counseling Zacchaeus, the young child laughed greatly and said: "Now let those bear fruit that were barren and let them see that were blind in heart. I am come from above that I may curse them, and call them to the things that are above, even as he commanded which hath sent me for your sakes." And when the young child ceased speaking, immediately all they were made whole which had come under his curse. And no man after that durst provoke him, lest he should curse him, and he should be maimed.

Now after certain days Jesus was playing in the upper story of a certain house, and one of the young children that played with him fell down from the house and died. And the other children when they saw it fled, and Jesus remained alone. And the parents of him that was dead came and accused him that he had cast him down. And Jesus said: "I did not cast him down" but they reviled him still. Then Jesus leaped down from the roof and stood by the body of the child and cried with a loud voice and said: "Zeno [for so was his name called], arise and tell me, did I cast thee down?" And straightway he arose and said: "Nay, Lord, thou didst not cast me down, but didst raise me up." And when they saw it they were amazed: and the parents of the child glorified God for the sign which had come to pass, and worshipped Jesus.

After a few days, a certain young man was cleaving wood in the neighborhood, and the axe fell and cut in sunder the sole of his foot, and losing much blood he was at the point to die. And when there was a tumult and concourse, the young child Jesus also ran thither, and by force passed through the multitude, and took hold upon the foot of the young man that was smitten, and straightway it was healed. And he said unto the young man: "Arise now and cleave the wood and remember me." But when the multitude saw what was done they worshipped the young child, saying: "Verily the spirit of God dwelleth in this young child."

Now when he was six years old, his mother sendeth him to draw water and bear it into the house, and gave him a pitcher: but in the press he struck it against another and the pitcher was broken. But Jesus spread out the garment which was upon him and filled it with water and brought it to his mother. And when his mother saw what was done she kissed him; and she kept within herself the mysteries which she saw him do.

Again, in the time of sowing the young child went forth with his father to sow wheat in their land: and as his father sowed, the young child Jesus sowed also one corn of wheat. And he reaped it and threshed it and made thereof a hundred measures: and he called all the poor of the village unto the threshing floor and gave them the wheat. And Joseph took the residue of the wheat. And he was eight years old when he wrought this sign.

Now his father was a carpenter and made at that time ploughs and yokes. And there was required of him a bed by a certain rich man, that he should make it for him. And whereas one beam, that which is called the shifting one, was too short and Joseph knew not what to do, the young child Jesus said to his father Joseph: "Lay down the two pieces of wood and make them even at the end next unto thee." And Joseph did as the young child said unto him. And Jesus stood at the other end and took hold upon the shorter beam and stretched it and made it equal with the other. And his father Joseph saw it and marveled: and he embraced the young child and kissed him, saying: "Happy am I for that God hath given me this young child."

But when Joseph saw the understanding of the child, and his age, that it was coming to the full, he thought with himself again that he should not be ignorant of letters; and he took him and delivered him to another teacher. And the teacher said unto Joseph: "First will I teach him the Greek letters, and after that the Hebrew." For the teacher knew the skill of the child and was afraid of him: notwithstanding he wrote the alphabet and Jesus pondered thereon a long time and answered him not. And Jesus said to him: "If thou be indeed a teacher and if thou knowest letters well, tell me the power of the Alpha and then will I tell thee the power of the Beta." And the teacher was provoked and smote him on the head. And the young child was hurt and cursed him, and straightway he fainted and fell to the ground on his face. And the child returned unto the house of Joseph: and Joseph was grieved and commanded his mother, saying: "Let him not forth without the door, for all they die that provoke him to wrath."

And after some time yet another teacher which was a faithful friend of Joseph said to him: "Bring the young child unto me to the school, peradventure I may be able by cockering him to teach him the letters." And Joseph said: "If thou hast no fear, my brother, take him with thee." And he took him with him, in fear and much trouble of spirit, but the young child followed him gladly. And going with boldness into the school he found a book lying upon the pulpit and he took it, and read not the letters that were therein, but opened his mouth and spake by the Holy Spirit, and taught the law to them that stood by. And a great multitude came together and stood there hearkening, and marveled at the beauty of his teaching and the readiness of his words, in that being an infant he uttered such things. But when Joseph heard it, he was afraid, and ran unto the school thinking whether this teacher also were without skill: but the teacher said unto Joseph: "Know, my brother, that I received this child for a disciple, but he is full of grace and wisdom; and now I beseech thee, brother, take him unto thine house." And when the young child heard that, he smiled upon him and said: "Forasmuch as thou hast said well and hast borne right witness, for thy sake shall he also that was smitten be healed." And forthwith the other teacher was healed. And Joseph took the young child and departed unto his house.

And Joseph sent his son James to bind fuel and carry it into his house. And the young child Jesus also followed him. And as James was gathering of faggots, a viper bit the hand of James. And as he was sore afflicted and ready to perish, Jesus came near and breathed upon the bite, and straightway the pain ceased, and the serpent burst, and forthwith James continued whole.

And after these things, in the neighborhood of Joseph, a little child fell sick and died, and his mother wept sore. And Jesus heard that there was great mourning and trouble and he ran quickly and found the child dead: and he touched his breast and said: "I say unto thee, Child, die not, but live and be with thy mother." And straightway it looked up and laughed. And he said to the woman: "Take him up and give him milk, and remember me." And the multitude that stood by saw it and marveled, and said: "Of a truth this young child is either a god or an angel of God; for every word of his is a perfect work." And Jesus departed thence, and was playing with other children.

And after some time there was work of building. And there came a great tumult, and Jesus arose and went thither: and he saw a man lying dead, and took hold of his hand and said: "Man, I say unto thee, arise and do thy work." And immediately he arose and worshipped him. And when the multitude saw it, they were astonished, and said: "This young child is from heaven: for he hath saved many souls from death, and hath power to save them all his life long."

And when he was twelve years old his parents went according to the custom unto Jerusalem to the feast of the Passover with their company: and after the Passover they returned to go unto their house. And as they returned the child Jesus went back to Jerusalem; but his parents supposed that he was in their company. And when they had gone a day's journey, they sought him among their kinsfolk, and when they found him not, they were troubled, and returned again to the city seeking him. And after the third day they found him in the temple sitting in the midst of the doctors and hearing and asking them questions. And all men paid heed to him and marveled how that being a young child he put to silence the elders and teachers of the people, expounding the heads of the law and the parables of the prophets. And his mother Mary came near and said unto him: "Child, wherefore hast thou so done unto us? Behold we have sought thee sorrowing." And Jesus said unto them: "Why seek ye me? know ye not that I must be in my Father's house?" But the scribes and Pharisees said: "Art thou the mother of this child?" and she said: "I am." And they said unto her: "Blessed art thou among women because God hath blessed the fruit of thy womb. For such glory and such excellence and wisdom we have neither seen nor heard at any time." And Jesus arose and followed his mother and was subject unto his parents: but his mother kept in mind all that came to pass. And Jesus increased in wisdom and stature and grace. Unto him be glory for ever and ever. Amen.

—*The Infancy Gospel of Thomas*

And He explained the books, and the law, and the precepts, and the statutes, and the mysteries, which are contained in the books of the prophets—things which the understanding of no creature attains to. That teacher therefore said: "I hitherto have neither attained to nor heard of such knowledge: Who, pray, do you think that boy will be?"

And a philosopher who was there present, a skillful astronomer, asked the Lord Jesus whether He had studied astronomy. And the Lord Jesus answered him, and explained the number of the spheres, and of the heavenly bodies, their natures and operations; their opposition; their aspect—triangular, square, and sextile; their course, direct and retrograde; the twenty-fourths, and sixtieths of twenty-fourths; and other things beyond the reach of reason.

There was also among those philosophers one very skilled in treating of natural science, and he asked the Lord Jesus whether He had studied medicine. And He, in reply, explained to him physics and metaphysics, hyperphysics and hypophysics, the powers likewise and humors of the body, and the effects of the same; also the number of members and bones, of veins, arteries, and nerves; also the effect of heat and dryness, of cold and moisture, and what these give rise to; what was the operation of the soul upon the body, and its perceptions and powers; what was the operation of the faculty of speech, of anger, of desire; lastly, their conjunction and disjunction, and other things beyond the reach of any created intellect. Then that philosopher rose up, and adored the Lord Jesus, and said: "O Lord, from this time I will be thy disciple and slave."

—*The Arabic Infancy Gospel*

"When thou wert little, before the spirit had come upon thee, whilst thou wert in a vineyard with Joseph, the spirit came out of the height and came to me in my house, like unto thee; and I had not known him, but I thought that thou wast he. And the spirit said unto me: 'Where is Jesus, my brother, that I meet with him?' And when he had said this unto me, I was at a loss and thought it was a phantom to try me. So I seized him and bound him to the foot of the bed in my house, until I went forth to you, to thee and Joseph in the field, and I found you on the vineyard, Joseph propping up the vineyard. It came to pass, therefore, when thou didst hear me speak the word unto Joseph, that thou didst understand the word, wert joyful and saidest: 'Where is he, that I may see him; else I await him in this place.' And it came to pass, when Joseph had heard thee say these words, that he was startled. And we went down together, entered the house and found the spirit bound to the bed. And we looked on thee and him and found thee like unto him. And he who was bound to the bed was unloosed; he took thee in his arms and kissed thee, and thou also didst kiss him. Ye became one."

—*The Pistis Sophia*

FOUR

The Person of Jesus

"The perfect Man"

Nowhere in the Bible is Jesus's appearance described. Yet in Christian art, he has consistently been depicted as pleasingly youthful and handsome—and often implausibly blond. Such features cohered with the doctrine of Jesus as God-made-man. To many Gnostics, however, Jesus was not a man at all; he was a spiritual being who merely appeared in human form.

And so, in Gnostic texts, this view is communicated with descriptions of a chameleon-like Christ whose appearance changes with startling speed. In the Secret Book of John, a Gnostic book that probably dates from the second century, was found in Nag Hammadi, and is also known as the Apocryphon of John, Jesus appears after his death as a youth, an old man, and a servant. In the Gospel of Philip, Jesus is variously great, small, and angelic-looking; sometimes he even appears to people as visions of themselves.

The Acts of John, a text with many Gnostic passages—though they may have been added after it was written in the second century—tells of the evangelizing of the disciple John. John tells us that Jesus has "many faces": childish, handsome, bald, small, and tall.

He never blinks, does not appear to leave footprints, and shifts between body and spirit.

Several texts that are not Gnostic also suggest that Jesus could mysteriously change his appearance. In the Acts of Peter, a first- or second-century book that describes the missionary work of the leader of the disciples, there are more visions of Jesus as an old man, a young man, and a boy. The Acts of Thomas, a second- or third-century book, describes Jesus, in a miraculous visitation, looking so much like his twin brother that he is taken for him. This is the book that tells the tale of how Thomas took Christianity to India after Jesus had sold him, rather ruthlessly, to the king of India as a carpenter.

The Acts of Peter and the Twelve Apostles, which was found in Nag Hammadi but is not a Gnostic work, contains a story of Jesus appearing disguised as a character called Lithargoel, a "beautiful" pearl seller, who later appears as a doctor. This book is thought to date from the early second century.

The Gnostic gospels also aim to describe Jesus's character. The Gospel of Truth, which was probably composed in the second century and is part of the Nag Hammadi Library, describes Jesus as a shepherd guiding his followers to the truth. Jesus's "kindly affection" is described in the Acts of John, while the Gospel of Philip includes a warm description of Jesus's goodness. Writers of non-Gnostic, noncanonical texts give similar descriptions. In the Acts of Peter, the disciple who in the

Bible thrice denies knowing Jesus says that Jesus forgave his error. In the Questions of Bartholomew, meanwhile, Jesus himself describes himself as "meek and gentle."

AND it happened one day, when John, the brother of James—who are the sons of Zebedee—had come up to the temple, that a Pharisee named Arimanius approached him and said to him, "Where is your master whom you followed?" And he said to him, "He has gone to the place from which he came." The Pharisee said to him, "With deception did this Nazarene deceive you, and he filled your ears with lies, and closed your hearts [and] turned you from the traditions of your fathers."

When I, John, heard these things I turned away from the temple to a desert place. And I grieved greatly in my heart, saying, "How then was the Savior appointed, and why was he sent into the world by his Father, and who is his Father who sent him, and of what sort is that aeon to which we shall go? For what did he mean when he said to us, 'This aeon to which you will go is of the type of the imperishable aeon,' but he did not teach us concerning the latter, of what sort it is."

Straightway, while I was contemplating these things, behold, the heavens opened and the whole creation which is below heaven shone, and the world was shaken. I was afraid, and behold I saw in the light a youth who stood by me. While I looked at him, he became like an old man. And he changed his likeness (again), becoming like a servant. There was not a plurality before me, but there was a likeness with multiple forms in the light, and the likenesses appeared through each other, and the likeness had three forms. He said to me, "John, John, why do you doubt, or why are you afraid? You are not unfamiliar with this image, are you?—that is, do not be timid!—I am the one who is with you always. I am the Father, I am the Mother, I am the Son. I am the undefiled and incorruptible one. Now I have come to teach you what is and what was and what will come to pass, that you may know the things which are not revealed and those which are revealed, and to teach you concerning the unwavering race of the perfect Man. Now, therefore, lift up your face, that you may receive the things that I shall teach you today, and may tell them to your fellow spirits who are from the unwavering race of the perfect Man."

—*The Secret Book of John*

Jesus took them all by stealth, for he did not reveal himself in the manner in which he was, but it was in the manner in which they would be able to see him that he revealed himself. He revealed himself to them all. He revealed himself as great to the great. He revealed himself as small to the small. He revealed himself to the angels as an angel. Because of this his word hid itself from everyone. Some indeed saw him, thinking that they were seeing themselves, but when he appeared to his disciples in glory on the mount he was not small. He became great, but he made the disciples great, that they might be able to see his greatness. He said on that day in the Thanksgiving, "You who have joined the perfect, the light, with the Holy Spirit, unite the angels with us also, the images. Do not despise the lamb, for without it, it is not possible to see the king."

—*The Gospel of Philip*

Men and brethren, ye have suffered nothing strange or incredible as concerning your perception of the Lord, inasmuch as we also, whom he chose for himself to be apostles, were tried in many ways: I, indeed, am neither able to set forth unto you nor to write the things which I both saw and heard: and now is it needful that I should fit them for your hearing; and according as each of you is able to contain it I will impart unto you those things whereof ye are able to become hearers, that ye may see the glory that is about him, which was and is, both now and for ever.

For when he had chosen Peter and Andrew, which were brethren, he cometh unto me and

James my brother, saying: "I have need of you, come unto me." And my brother hearing that, said: "John, what would this child have that is upon the sea-shore and called us?" And I said: "What child?" And he said to me again: "That which beckoneth to us." And I answered: "Because of our long watch we have kept at sea, thou seest not aright, my brother James; but seest thou not the man that standeth there, comely and fair and of a cheerful countenance?" But he said to me: "Him I see not, brother; but let us go forth and we shall see what he would have."

And so when we had brought the ship to land, we saw him also helping along with us to settle the ship: and when we departed from that place, being minded to follow him, again he was seen of me as having [a head] rather bald, but the beard thick and flowing, but of James as a youth whose beard was newly come. We were therefore perplexed, both of us, as to what that which we had seen should mean. And after that, as we followed him, both of us were by little and little perplexed as we considered the matter. Yet unto me there then appeared this yet more wonderful thing: for I would try to see him privily, and I never at any time saw his eyes closing [blinking], but only open. And ofttimes he would appear to me as a small man and uncomely, and then again as one reaching unto heaven. Also there was in him another marvel:

when I sat at meat he would take me upon his own breast; and sometimes his breast was felt of me to be smooth and tender, and sometimes hard like unto stones, so that I was perplexed in myself and said: "Wherefore is this so unto me?"

And at another time he taketh with him me and James and Peter unto the mountain where he was wont to pray, and we saw in him a light such as it is not possible for a man that useth corruptible speech to describe what it was like. Again in like manner he bringeth us three up into the mountain, saying: "Come ye with me." And we went again: and we saw him at a distance praying. I, therefore, because he loved me, drew nigh unto him softly, as though he could not see me, and stood looking upon his hinder parts: and I saw that he was not in any wise clad with garments, but was seen of us naked, and not in any wise as a man, and that his feet were whiter than any snow, so that the earth there was lighted up by his feet, and that his head touched the heaven: so that I was afraid and cried out, and he, turning about, appeared as a man of small stature, and caught hold on my beard and pulled it and said to me: "John, be not faithless but believing, and not curious." And I said unto him: "But what have I done, Lord?" And I say unto you, brethren, I suffered so great pain in that place where he took hold on my beard for thirty days, that I said to him: "Lord, if thy twitch when thou wast in sport hath given me so great pain, what were it if thou hadst given me a buffet?" And he said unto me: "Let it be thine henceforth not to tempt him that cannot be tempted."

But Peter and James were wroth because I spake with the Lord, and beckoned unto me that I should come unto them and leave the Lord alone. And I went, and they both said unto me: "He that was speaking with the Lord upon the top of the mount, who was he?" For we heard both of them speaking. And I, having in mind his great grace, and his unity which hath many faces, and his wisdom which without ceasing looketh upon us, said: "That shall ye learn if ye inquire of him."

Again, once when all we his disciples were at Gennesaret sleeping in one house, I alone having wrapped myself in my mantle, watched what he should do: and first I heard him say: "John, go thou to sleep." And I thereon feigning to sleep saw another like unto him, whom also I heard say unto my Lord: "Jesus, they whom thou hast chosen believe not yet on thee." And my Lord said unto him: "Thou sayest well: for they are men."

Another glory also will I tell you, brethren: Sometimes when I would lay hold on him, I met with a material and solid body, and at other times, again, when I felt him, the substance was immaterial and as if it existed not at all. And if at any time he were bidden by some one of the Pharisees and went to the bidding, we went with him, and there was set before each one of us a loaf by them that had bidden us, and with us he also received one; and his own he would bless and part it among us: and of that little every one was filled, and our own loaves were saved whole, so that they which bade him were amazed. And oftentimes when I walked with him, I desired to see the print of his foot, whether it appeared on the earth; for I saw him as it were lifting himself up from the earth: and I never saw it. And these things I speak unto you, brethren, for the encouragement of your faith toward him; for we must at the present keep silence concerning his mighty and wonderful works, inasmuch as they are unspeakable and, it may be, cannot at all be either uttered or heard.

—*The Acts of John*

Our Lord, willing that I should behold his majesty in the holy mount—I, when I with the sons of Zebedee saw the brightness of his light, fell as one dead and shut mine eyes, and heard such a voice from him as I am not able to describe, and thought myself to be blinded by his brightness. And when I recovered a little I said within myself: "Peradventure my Lord hath brought me hither that he might blind me." And I said: "If this also be thy will, Lord, I resist not." And he gave me his hand and raised me up; and when I arose I saw him again in such a form as I was able to take in. As, therefore, the merciful God, dearly beloved brethren, carried our infirmities and bare our sins (as the prophet saith: "He beareth our sins and suffereth for us; but we did esteem him to be in affliction and smitten with plagues"), for he is in the Father and the Father in him—he also is himself the fullness of all majesty, who hath shown unto us all his good things: he did eat and drink for our sakes, himself being neither ahungered nor athirst; he carried and bore reproaches for our sakes; he died and rose again because of us; who both defended me when I sinned and comforted me by his greatness, and will comfort you also that ye may love him: this God who is great and small, fair and foul, young and old, seen in time and unto eternity invisible; whom the hand of man hath not held, yet is he held by his servants; whom no flesh hath seen, yet now seeth; who is the word proclaimed by the prophets and now appearing; not subject to suffering, but having now made trial of suffering for our sake; never chastised, yet now chastised; who was before the world and hath been comprehended in time; the great beginning of all principality, yet delivered over unto princes; beautiful, but among us lowly; seen of all yet foreseeing all. This Jesus ye have, brethren, the door, the light, the way, the bread, the water, the life, the resurrection, the refreshment, the pearl, the treasure, the seed, the abundance, the mustard seed, the vine, the plough, the grace, the faith, the word: he is all things and there is none other greater than he. Unto him be praise, world without end. Amen.

. . .

And when the ninth hour was fully come, they rose up to make prayer. And behold certain widows, of the aged, unknown to Peter, which sat there, being blind and not believing, cried out, saying unto Peter: "We sit together here, O Peter, hoping and believing in Christ Jesus: as therefore thou hast made one of us to see, we entreat thee, lord Peter, grant unto us also his mercy and pity." But Peter said to them: "If there be in you the faith that is in Christ, if it be firm in you, then perceive in your mind that which ye see not with your eyes, and though your ears are closed, yet let them be open in your mind within you. These eyes shall again be shut, seeing naught but men and oxen and dumb beasts and stones and sticks; but not every eye seeth Jesus Christ. Yet now, Lord, let thy sweet and holy name succor these persons; do thou touch their eyes; for thou art able—that these may see with their eyes."

And when all had prayed, the hall wherein they were shone as when it lighteneth, even with such a light as cometh in the clouds, yet not such a light as that of the daytime, but unspeakable, invisible, such as no man can describe, even such that we were beside ourselves with bewilderment, calling on the Lord and saying: "Have mercy, Lord, upon us thy servants: what we are able to bear, that, Lord, give thou us; for this we can neither see nor endure." And as we lay there, only those widows stood up which were blind; and the bright light which appeared unto us entered into their eyes and made them to see. Unto whom Peter said: "Tell us what ye saw." And they said: "We saw an old man of such comeliness as we are not able to declare to thee"; but others said: "We saw a young man"; and others: "We saw a boy touching our eyes delicately, and so were our eyes opened." Peter therefore magnified the Lord, saying: "Thou only art the Lord God, and of what lips have we need to give thee due praise? And how can we give thee thanks according to thy mercy?" Therefore, brethren, as I told you but a little while since, God that is constant is greater than our thoughts, even as we have learned of these aged widows, how that they beheld the Lord in divers forms.

—*The Acts of Peter*

At that season all we the apostles were at Jerusalem, Simon which is called Peter and Andrew his brother, James the son of Zebedee and John his brother, Philip and Bartholomew, Thomas and Matthew the publican, James the son of Alphaeus and Simon the Canaanite, and Judas the brother of James: and we divided the regions of the world, that every one of us should go unto the region that fell to him and unto the nation whereunto the Lord sent him.

According to the lot, therefore, India fell unto Judas Thomas, which is also the twin: but he would not go, saying that by reason of the weakness of the flesh he could not travel, and "I am an Hebrew man; how can I go amongst the Indians and preach the truth?" And as he thus reasoned and spake, the Savior appeared unto him by night and saith to him: "Fear not, Thomas, go thou unto India and preach the word there, for my grace is with thee." But he would not obey, saying: "Whither thou wouldest send me, send me, but elsewhere, for unto the Indians I will not go."

And while he thus spake and thought, it chanced that there was there a certain merchant come from India whose name was Abbanes, sent from the King Gundaphorus, and having commandment from him to buy a carpenter and bring him unto him.

Now the Lord seeing him walking in the marketplace at noon said unto him: "Wouldest thou buy a carpenter?" And he said to him: "Yea." And the Lord said to him: "I have a slave that is a carpenter and I desire to sell him." And so saying he showed him Thomas afar off, and agreed with him for three litrae of silver unstamped, and wrote a deed of sale, saying: "I, Jesus, the son of Joseph the carpenter, acknowledge that I have sold my slave, Judas by name, unto thee Abbanes, a merchant of Gundaphorus, king of the Indians." And when the deed was finished, the Savior took Judas Thomas and led him away to Abbanes the merchant, and when Abbanes saw him he said unto him: "Is this thy master?" And the apostle said: "Yea, he is my Lord." And he said: "I have bought thee of him." And thy apostle held his peace.

And on the day following the apostle arose early, and having prayed and besought the Lord he said: "I will go whither thou wilt, Lord Jesus: thy will be done." And he departed unto Abbanes the merchant, taking with him nothing at all save only his price. For the Lord had given it unto him, saying: "Let thy price also be with thee, together with my grace, wheresoever thou goest."

And the apostle found Abbanes carrying his baggage on board the ship; so he also began to carry it aboard with him. And when they were embarked in the ship and were set down Abbanes questioned the apostle, saying: "What craftsmanship knowest thou?" And he said: "In wood I can make ploughs and yokes and augers, and boats and oars for boats and masts and pulleys; and in stone, pillars and temples and courthouses for kings."

And Abbanes the merchant said to him: "Yea, it is of such a workman that we have need." They began then to sail homeward; and they had a favorable wind, and sailed prosperously till they reached Andrapolis, a royal city.

And they left the ship and entered into the city, and lo, there were noises of flutes and water-organs, and trumpets sounded about them; and the apostle inquired, saying: "What is this festival that is in this city?" And they that were there said to him: "Thee also have the gods brought to make merry in this city. For the king hath an only daughter, and now he giveth her in marriage unto a husband: this rejoicing, therefore, and assembly of the wedding today is the festival which thou hast seen. And the king hath sent heralds to proclaim everywhere that all should come to the marriage, rich and poor, bond and free, strangers and citizens: and if any refuse and come not to the marriage he shall answer for it unto the king." And Abbanes hearing that said to the apostle: "Let us also go, lest we offend the king, especially seeing we are strangers." And he said: "Let us go."

And after they had put up in the inn and rested a little space they went to the marriage; and the apostle seeing them all set down (reclining), laid himself, he also, in the midst, and all looked upon him, as upon a stranger and one come from a foreign land: but Abbanes the merchant, being his master, laid himself in another place.

. . .

And the king desired the groomsmen to depart out of the bride-chamber; and when all were gone out and the doors were shut, the bridegroom lifted up the curtain of the bride-chamber to fetch the bride unto him. And he saw the Lord Jesus bearing the likeness of Judas Thomas and speaking with the bride; even of him that but now had blessed them and gone out from them, the apostle; and he saith unto him: "Wentest thou not out in the sight of all? how then art thou found here?" But the Lord said to him: "I am not Judas which is also called Thomas but I am his brother."

—*The Acts of Thomas*

We went down to the sea at an opportune moment, which came to us from the Lord. We found a ship moored at the shore ready to embark, and we spoke with the sailors of the ship about our coming aboard with them. They showed great kindliness toward us as was ordained by the Lord. And after we had embarked, we sailed a day and a night. After that, a wind came up behind the ship and brought us to a small city in the midst of the sea.

And I, Peter, inquired about the name of this city from residents who were standing on the dock.

A man among them answered, saying, "The name of this city is Habitation, that is [. . .] endurance. . . ." And after we had gone ashore with the baggage, I went into the city, to seek advice about lodging.

A man came out wearing a cloth bound around his waist, and a gold belt girded it. Also a napkin was tied over his chest, extending over his shoulders and covering his head and his hands.

I was staring at the man, because he was beautiful in his form and stature. There were four parts of his body that I saw: the soles of his feet and a part of his chest and the palms of his hands and his visage. These things I was able to see. A book cover like [those of] my books was in his left hand. A staff of styrax wood was in his right hand. His voice was resounding as he slowly spoke, crying out in the city, "Pearls! Pearls!"

I, indeed, thought he was a man of that city. I said to him, "My brother and my friend!" He answered me, then, saying, "Rightly did you say, 'My brother and my friend.' What is it you seek from me?" I said to him, "I ask you about lodging for me and the brothers also, because we are strangers here." He said to me, "For this reason have I myself just said, 'My brother and my friend,' because I also am a fellow stranger like you."

And having said these things, he cried out, "Pearls! Pearls!" The rich men of that city heard his voice. They came out of their hidden storerooms. And some were looking out from the storerooms of their houses. Others looked out from their upper windows. And they did not see [that they could gain] anything from him, because there was no pouch on his back nor bundle inside his cloth and napkin. And because of their disdain they did not even acknowledge him. He, for his part, did not reveal himself to them. They returned to their storerooms, saying, "This man is mocking us."

And the poor of that city heard his voice, and they came to the man who sells this pearl. They said, "Please take the trouble to show us the pearl so that we may, then, see it with our [own] eyes. For we are the poor. And we do not have this [. . .] price to pay for it. But show us that we might say to our friends that we saw a pearl with our [own] eyes." He answered, saying to them, "If it is possible, come to my city, so that I may not only show it before your [very] eyes, but give it to you for nothing."

And indeed they, the poor of that city, heard and said, "Since we are beggars, we surely know that a man does not give a pearl to a beggar, but [it is] bread and money that is usually received. Now then, the kindness which we want to receive from you [is] that you show us the pearl before our eyes. And we will say to our friends proudly that we saw a pearl with our [own] eyes"—because it is not found among the poor, especially such beggars [as these]. He answered [and] said to them, "If it is possible, you yourselves come to my city, so that I may not only show you it, but give it to you for nothing." The poor and the beggars rejoiced because of the man who gives for nothing.

The men asked Peter about the hardships. Peter answered and told those things that he had heard about the hardships of the way. Because they are interpreters of the hardships in their ministry.

He said to the man who sells this pearl, "I want to know your name and the hardships of the way to your city because we are strangers and servants of God. It is necessary for us to spread the word of God in every city harmoniously." He answered and said, "If you seek my name, Lithargoel is my name, the interpretation of which is, the light, gazelle-like stone.

"And also [concerning] the road to the city, which you asked me about, I will tell you about it. No man is able to go on that road, except one who has forsaken everything that he has and has fasted daily from stage to stage. For many are the robbers and wild beasts on that road. The one who carries bread with him on the road, the black dogs kill because of the bread. The one who carries a costly garment of the world with him, the robbers kill because of the garment. The one who carries water with him, the wolves kill because of the water, since they are thirsty for it. The one who is anxious about meat and green vegetables, the lions eat because of the meat. If he evades the lions, the bulls devour him because of the green vegetables."

When he had said these things to me, I sighed within myself, saying, "Great hardships are on the road! If only Jesus would give us power to walk it!" He looked at me since my face was sad, and I sighed. He said to me, "Why do you sigh, if you, indeed, know this name 'Jesus' and believe him? He is a great power for giving strength. For I too believe in the Father who sent him."

I replied, asking him, "What is the name of the place to which you go, your city?" He said to me, "This is the name of my city, 'Nine Gates.' Let us praise God as we are mindful that the tenth is the head." After this I went away from him in peace.

As I was about to go and call my friends, I saw waves and large high walls surrounding the bounds of the city. I marveled at the great things I saw. I saw an old man sitting and I asked him if the name of the city was really Habitation. He [. . .], "Habitation [. . .]." He said to me, "You speak truly, for we inhabit here because we endure."

I responded, saying, "Justly [. . .] have men named it [. . .], because [by] everyone who endures his trials, cities are inhabited, and a precious kingdom comes from them, because they endure in the midst of the apostasies and the difficulties of the storms. So that in this way, the city of everyone who endures the burden of his yoke of faith will be inhabited, and he will be included in the kingdom of heaven."

I hurried and went and called my friends so that we might go to the city that he, Lithargoel, appointed for us. In a bond of faith we forsook everything as he had said [to do]. We evaded the robbers, because they did not find their garments with us. We evaded the wolves, because they did not find the water with us for which they thirsted. We evaded the lions, because they did not find the desire for meat with us. We evaded the bulls [. . .] they did not find green vegetables.

A great joy came upon us and a peaceful carefreeness like that of our Lord. We rested ourselves in front of the gate, and we talked with each other about that which is not a distraction of this world. Rather we continued in contemplation of the faith.

As we discussed the robbers on the road, whom we evaded, behold Lithargoel, having changed, came out to us. He had the appearance of a physician, since an unguent box was under his arm, and a young disciple was following him carrying a pouch full of medicine. We did not recognize him.

Peter responded and said to him, "We want you to do us a favor, because we are strangers, and take us to the house of Lithargoel before evening comes." He said, "In uprightness of heart I will show it to you. But I am amazed at how you knew this good man. For he does not reveal himself to every man, because he himself is the son of a great king. Rest yourselves a little so that I may go and heal this man and come [back]." He hurried and came [back] quickly.

He said to Peter, "Peter!" And Peter was frightened, for how did he know that his name was Peter? Peter responded to the Savior, "How do you know me, for you called my name?" Lithargoel answered, "I want to ask you who gave the name Peter to you?" He said to him, "It was Jesus Christ, the son of the living God. He gave this name to me." He answered and said, "It is I! Recognize me, Peter." He loosened the garment, which clothed him—the one into which he had changed himself because of us—revealing to us in truth that it was he.

We prostrated ourselves on the ground and worshipped him. We comprised eleven disciples. He stretched forth his hand and caused us to stand. We spoke with him humbly. Our heads were bowed down in unworthiness as we said, "What you wish we will do. But give us power to do what you wish at all times."

He gave them the unguent box and the pouch that was in the hand of the young disciple. He commanded them like this, saying, "Go into the city from which you came, which is called Habitation. Continue in endurance as you teach all those who have believed in my name, because I have endured in hardships of the faith. I will give you your reward. To the poor of that city give what they need in order to live until I give them what is better, which I told you that I will give you for nothing."

Peter answered and said to him, "Lord, you have taught us to forsake the world and everything in it. We have renounced them for your sake. What we are concerned about [now] is the food for a single day. Where will we be able to find the needs that you ask us to provide for the poor?"

The Lord answered and said, "O Peter, it was necessary that you understand the parable that I told you! Do you not understand that my name, which you teach, surpasses all riches, and the wisdom of God surpasses gold, and silver and precious stone(s)?"

He gave them the pouch of medicine and said, "Heal all the sick of the city who believe in my name." Peter was afraid to reply to him for the second time. He signaled to the one who was beside him, who was John: "You talk this time." John answered and said, "Lord, before you we are afraid to say many words. But it is you who asks us to practice this skill. We have not been taught to be physicians. How then will we know how to heal bodies as you have told us?"

He answered them, "Rightly have you spoken, John, for I know that the physicians of this world heal what belongs to the world. The physicians of souls, however, heal the heart. Heal the bodies first, therefore, so that through the real powers of healing for their bodies, without the medicine of the world, they may believe in you, that you have power to heal the illnesses of the heart also.

"The rich men of the city, however, those who did not see fit even to acknowledge me, but who reveled in their wealth and pride—with such as these, therefore, do not dine in their houses nor be friends with them, lest their partiality influence you. For many in the churches have shown partiality to the rich, because they also are sinful, and they give occasion for others to sin. But judge them with uprightness, so that your ministry may be glorified, and that my name also, may be glorified in the churches." The disciples answered and said, "Yes, truly this is what is fitting to do."

They prostrated themselves on the ground and worshipped him. He caused them to stand and departed from them in peace. Amen.

—*The Acts of Peter and the Twelve Apostles*

When he had appeared, instructing them about the Father, the incomprehensible one, when he had breathed into them what is in the thought, doing his will, when many had received the light, they turned to him. For the material ones were strangers, and did not see his likeness, and had not known him. For he came by means of fleshly form, while nothing blocked his course, because incorruptibility is irresistible, since he, again, spoke new things, still speaking about what is in the heart of the Father, having brought forth the flawless Word.

When light had spoken through his mouth, as well as his voice, which gave birth to life, he gave them thought and understanding, and mercy and salvation, and the powerful spirit from the infiniteness and the sweetness of the Father. Having made punishments and tortures cease—for it was they which were leading astray from his face some who were in need of mercy, in error and in bonds—he both destroyed them with power and confounded them with knowledge. He became a way for those who were gone astray, and knowledge for those who were ignorant, a discovery for those who were searching, and a support for those who were wavering, immaculateness for those who were defiled.

He is the shepherd who left behind the ninety-nine sheep which were not lost. He went searching for the one which had gone astray.

—*The Gospel of Truth*

Having therefore beheld, brethren, the grace of the Lord and his kindly affection toward us, let us worship him as those unto whom he hath shown mercy, not with our fingers, nor our mouth, nor our tongue, nor with any part whatsoever of our body, but with the disposition of our soul—even him who became a man apart from this body: and let us watch because now also he keepeth ward over prisons for our sake, and over tombs, in bonds and dungeons, in reproaches and insults, by sea and on dry land, in scourgings, condemnations, conspiracies, frauds, punishments, and in a word, he is with all of us, and himself suffereth with us when we suffer, brethren. . . .

Be ye also persuaded, therefore, beloved, that it is not a man whom I preach unto you to worship, but God unchangeable, God invincible, God higher than all authority and all power, and elder and mightier than all angels and creatures that are named, and all aeons. If then ye abide in him, and are builded up in him, ye shall possess your soul indestructible.

—*The Acts of John*

Blessed is the one who on no occasion caused a soul distress. That person is Jesus Christ. He came to the whole place and did not burden anyone. Therefore the blessed is the one who is like this, because he is a perfect man.

—*The Gospel of Philip*

And as Bartholomew thus spake again, Jesus put off his mantle and took a kerchief from the neck of Bartholomew and began to rejoice and say: "I am good. Alleluia. I am meek and gentle. Alleluia. Glory be to thee, O Lord: for I give gifts unto all them that desire me. Alleluia. Glory be to thee, O Lord, world without end. Amen. Alleluia." And when he had ceased, the apostles kissed him, and he gave them the peace of love.

—*The Questions of Bartholomew*

I do confess, dearly beloved brethren, that I was with him: yet I denied him, even our Lord Jesus Christ, and that not once only, but thrice; for there were evil dogs that were come about me as they did unto the Lord's prophets. And the Lord imputed it not unto me, but turned unto me and had compassion on the infirmity of my flesh, when [or so that] afterward I bitterly bewailed myself, and lamented the weakness of my faith, because I was befooled by the devil and kept not in mind the word of my Lord.

—*The Acts of Peter*

FIVE

Mary Magdalene

"The companion of the Savior"

In the biblical gospel of John, Mary Magdalene, from the city of Magdala on the western coast of the Sea of Galilee, has an important role: it is she who finds Jesus's tomb empty three days after the crucifixion and who later mistakes the risen Lord for a gardener. But aside from this, in the Bible Mary Magdalene says very little.

In the Gnostic books, she steps out of the shadows. Talkative and clever, she almost dominates many conversations between Jesus and his disciples—of whom she is clearly a member. Many of these texts also suggest, at the least, that Jesus was particularly fond of her. In the Gospel of Philip, in which Mary Magdalene is described as his "companion," it is said that Jesus often kissed her, to the annoyance of his disciples.

The relationship causes jealousy, too, in the second-century Gospel of Mary. The first six pages of this book are missing, but much of what remains is in the form of Mary Magdalene relaying to the disciples a conversation she had with Jesus after his death. When Mary has finished telling them what Jesus told her—a long, Gnostic explanation of the soul's journey to heaven—she is challenged by the apostles Andrew and Peter, who doubt that Jesus would have confided in her. She weeps, and the apostle Levi comes to her defense, pointing out that Jesus "loved her more than us."

Mary asks Jesus many theological questions in the Sophia of Jesus Christ. This is an adaptation of another work: Eugonostos the Blessed. Both are in the Nag Hammadi Library and are probably among the oldest of these texts. In the Pistis Sophia, Mary Magdalene is responsible for thirty-nine of the forty-six questions put to Jesus in the book. In the presence of other disciples, Jesus congratulates Mary on her perspicacity. He says her "heart is raised to the kingdom of heaven more than all thy brethren." This seems to rile Peter, who then accuses Mary of monopolizing the conversation; she fires back, accusing him of sexism: he "hateth our sex." Theologians have wondered to what degree this fractious relationship between Mary Magdalene and Peter reflects tensions over the role of women in the early Church.

In the Dialogue of the Savior, Mary Magdalene again seems to ask all the right questions of Jesus, understands his cryptic replies, and is described as "a woman who had understood completely." This book, part of the Nag Hammadi Library, is badly damaged, with many words missing. It probably dates from the second century.

The Gospel of John's account of Mary meeting Jesus after his resurrection is turned into a poem in the Manichaean Psalms of Heracleides, which are thought to date from the third or fourth century. Mani, the third-century founder of Manichaeanism—a religion incorporating Christian, Zoroastrian, and Buddhist ideas—believed, like the Gnostics, that matter was corrupt.

Despite their fascination with Mary Magdalene, Gnostic writers were not feminists. The Gospel of Thomas gives another instance of Peter challenging Mary. When he asks Jesus to eject Mary from the group, Jesus says he will, instead, "make her male."

THERE were three who always walked with the Lord: Mary, his mother, and his sister and Magdalene, the one who was his companion. His sister and his mother and his companion were each a Mary.

. . .

And the companion of the [. . .] Mary Magdalene. [. . . loved] her more than all the disciples and used to kiss her often on the [. . .]. The rest of the disciples [. . .] They said to him, "Why do you love her more than all of us?" The Savior answered and said to them, "Why do I not love you like her? When a blind man and one who sees are both together in darkness, they are no different from one another. When the light comes, then he who sees will see the light, and he who is blind will remain in darkness."

—*The Gospel of Philip*

But they were grieved. They wept greatly, saying, "How shall we go to the Gentiles and preach the gospel of the kingdom of the Son of Man? If they did not spare him, how will they spare us?" Then Mary stood up, greeted them all, and said to her brethren, "Do not weep and do not grieve nor be irresolute, for his grace will be entirely with you and will protect you. But rather let us praise his greatness, for he has prepared us and turned us into men." When Mary said this she turned their hearts to the good and they began to discuss the words of the Savior.

Peter said to Mary, "Sister, we know that the Savior loved you more than the rest of women. Tell us the words of the Savior that you remember—which you know but we do not, nor have we heard them." And Mary answered and said, "What is hidden from you I will proclaim to you."

And she began to speak to them these words: "I," she said, "I saw the Lord in a vision and I said to Him, 'Lord, I saw you today in a vision.' He answered and said to me, 'Blessed are you that you did not waver at the sight of Me. For where the mind is there is the treasure.'

"I said to Him, 'Lord, how does he who sees the vision see it, through the soul or through the spirit?'

"The Savior answered and said, 'He does not see through the soul nor through the spirit, but the mind that is between the two, that is what sees the vision and it is [. . .].'"

[pages 11–14 are missing from the manuscript]

"And desire said, 'I did not see you descending, but now I see you ascending. Why do you lie since you belong to me?'

"The soul answered and said, 'I saw you. You did not see me nor recognize me. I served you as a garment and you did not know me.'

"When it said this, it [the soul] went away rejoicing greatly.

"Again it came to the third power, which is called ignorance.

"The power questioned the soul, saying, 'Where are you going? In wickedness are you bound. But you are bound; do not judge!'

"And the soul said, 'Why do you judge me, although I have not judged?'

"I was bound, though I have not bound.

"I was not recognized. But I have recognized that the All is being dissolved, both the earthly things and the heavenly.

"When the soul had overcome the third power, it went upward and saw the fourth power, which took seven forms.

"The first form is darkness, the second desire, the third ignorance, the fourth is the excitement of death, the fifth is the kingdom of the flesh, the sixth is the foolish wisdom of flesh, the seventh is the wrathful wisdom. These are the seven powers of wrath.

"They asked the soul, 'Whence do you come slayer of men, or where are you going, conqueror of space?'

"The soul answered and said, 'What binds me has been slain, and what turns me about has been overcome, and my desire has been ended, and ignorance has died.

"'In an aeon I was released from a world, and in a Type from a type, and from the fetter of oblivion which is transient.

"'From this time on will I attain to the rest of the time, of the season, of the aeon, in silence.'"

When Mary had said this, she fell silent, since it was to this point that the Savior had spoken with her. But Andrew answered and said to the brethren, "Say what you wish to say about what she has said. I at least do not believe that the Savior said this. For certainly these teachings are strange ideas." Peter answered and spoke concerning these same things. He questioned them about the Savior. "Did he really speak with a woman without our knowledge and not openly? Are we to turn about and all listen to her? Did he prefer her to us?"

Then Mary wept and said to Peter, "My brother

Peter, what do you think? Do you think that I thought this up myself in my heart, or that I am lying about the Savior?" Levi answered and said to Peter, "Peter, you have always been hot-tempered. Now I see you contending against the woman like the adversaries. But if the Savior made her worthy, who are you indeed to reject her? Surely the Savior knows her very well. That is why he loved her more than us. Rather let us be ashamed and put on the perfect man and acquire for ourselves as he commanded and preach the gospel, not laying down any other rule or law beyond what the Savior said."

—*The Gospel of Mary*

He called out, saying: "Whoever has ears to hear about the infinities, let him hear" and, "I have addressed those who are awake." Still he continued and said: "Everything that came from the perishable will perish, since it came from the perishable. But whatever came from imperishableness does not perish but becomes imperishable. So, many men went astray because they had not known this difference and they died."

Mary said to him: "Lord, then how will we know that?" The Perfect Savior said: "Come from invisible things to the end of those that are visible, and the very emanation of Thought will reveal to you how faith in those things that are not visible was found in those that are visible, those that belong to Unbegotten Father. Whoever has ears to hear, let him hear."

. . .

Mary said to him: "Holy Lord, where did your disciples come from, and where are they going, and [what] should they do here?" The Perfect Savior said to them: "I want you to know that Sophia, the Mother of the Universe and the consort, desired by herself to bring these to existence without her male [consort]."

—*The Sophia of Jesus Christ*

When then he had said this to his disciples, he said unto them: "Who hath ears to hear, let him hear."

It came to pass then, when Mary had heard the Savior say these words, that she gazed fixedly into the air for the space of an hour. She said: "My Lord, give commandment unto me to speak in openness."

And Jesus, the compassionate, answered and said unto Mary: "Mary, thou blessed one, whom I will perfect in all mysteries of those of the height, discourse in openness, thou, whose heart is raised to the kingdom of heaven more than all thy brethren."

Then said Mary to the Savior: "My Lord, the word which thou hast spoken unto us: 'Who hath ears to hear, let him hear,' thou sayest in order that we may understand the word which thou hast spoken. Hearken, therefore, my Lord, that I may discourse in openness.

"The words which thou hast spoken: 'I have taken a third from the power of the rulers of all the aeons, and changed their Fate and their sphere over which they rule, in order that, if the race of men invoke them in the mysteries—those which the angels who transgressed have taught them for the accomplishing of their evil and lawless deeds in the mystery of their sorcery,'—in order then that they may no more from this hour accomplish their lawless deeds, because thou hast taken their power from them and from their horoscope-casters and their consulters and from those who declare to the men in the world all things which shall come to pass, in order that they should no more from this hour know how to declare unto them any thing at all which will come to pass [for thou hast changed their spheres, and hast made them spend six months turned to the left and accomplishing their influences, and another six months facing the right and accomplishing their influences],—concerning this word then, my Lord, the power which was in the prophet Isaiah, hath spoken thus and proclaimed aforetime in a spiritual similitude, discoursing on the 'Vision about Egypt': 'Where then, O Egypt, where are thy consulters and horoscope-casters and those who cry out of the earth and those who cry out of their belly? Let them then declare unto thee from now on the deeds which the lord Sabao–th will do!'

"The power then which was in the prophet Isaiah, prophesied before thou didst come, that thou wouldst take away the power of the rulers of the aeons and wouldst change their sphere and their Fate, in order that they might know nothing from now on. For this cause it hath said also: 'Ye shall then know not of what the lord Sabao–th will do,' that is, none of the rulers will know what thou wilt do from now on,—for they are 'Egypt,' because they are matter. The power then which was in Isaiah, prophesied concerning thee aforetime, saying: 'From now on ye shall then know not what the lord Sabao–th will do.' Because of the light-power which thou didst receive from Sabao–th, the Good, who is in the region of the Right, and which is in thy material body today, for this cause then, my Lord Jesus, thou hast said unto us: 'Who hath ears to hear, let him hear,'—in order that thou mightest know whose heart is ardently raised to the kingdom of heaven."

. . .

It came to pass then, when Jesus had finished speaking these words unto his disciples, that he said unto them: "Do ye understand in what manner I discourse with you?"

And Peter started forward and said unto Jesus: "My Lord, we will not endure this woman, for she taketh the opportunity from us and hath let none of us speak, but she discourseth many times."

And Jesus answered and said unto his disciples: "Let him in whom the power of his spirit shall seethe, so that he understandeth what I say, come forward and speak. But now, Peter, I see thy power in thee, that it understandeth the solution of the mystery of the repentance which Pistis Sophia hath uttered. Now, therefore, Peter, speak the thought of her repentance in the midst of thy brethren."

It came to pass then, when the First Mystery had finished speaking these words unto the disciples, that Mary came forward and said: "My Lord, my mind is ever understanding, at every time to come forward and set forth the solution of the words which she hath uttered; but I am afraid of Peter, because he threatened me and hateth our sex."

And when she had said this, the First Mystery said unto her: "Every one who shall be filled with the spirit of light to come forward and set forth the solution of what I say,—no one shall be able to prevent him. Now, therefore, O Mary, set forth then the solution of the words which Pistis Sophia hath uttered."

. . .

It came to pass then, when Jesus had finished speaking these words, that Mary Magdalene started forward and said:

"My Lord, my indweller of light hath ears and I comprehend every word which thou sayest. Now, therefore, my Lord, on account of the word which thou hast spoken: 'All the souls of the race of men who shall receive the mysteries of the Light, will go into the Inheritance of the Light before all the rulers who will repent, and before those of the whole region of the Right and before the whole region of the Treasury of the Light,'—on account of this word, my Lord, thou hast said unto us aforetime: 'The first will be last and the last will be first,'—that is, the 'last' are the whole race of men which will enter into the Light-kingdom sooner than all those of the region of the Height, who are the first. On this account, therefore, my Lord, hast thou said unto us: 'Who hath ears to hear, let him hear,'—that is thou desirest to know whether we comprehend every word which thou speakest. This, therefore, is the word, my Lord."

It came to pass then, when Mary had finished saying these words, that the Savior was greatly astonished at the definitions of the words which she spake, for she had become pure spirit utterly. Jesus answered again and said unto her: "Well said, spiritual and pure Mary. This is the solution of the word."

—*The Pistis Sophia*

Mary hailed her brethren . . .

. . .

Then he [. . .] Judas and Matthew and Mary [. . .] the edge of heaven and earth. And when he placed his hand upon them, they hoped that they might [. . .] it. Judas raised his eyes and saw an exceedingly high place, and he saw the place of the abyss below.

. . .

Mary said, "Thus with respect to 'the wickedness of each day,' and 'the laborer is worthy of his food,' and 'the disciple resembles his teacher.'" She uttered this as a woman who had understood completely.

. . .

Mary said, "Tell me, Lord, why I have come to this place to profit or to forfeit." The Lord said, "You make clear the abundance of the revealer!" Mary said to him, "Lord, is there then a place which is [. . .] or lacking truth?" The Lord said, "The place where I am not!" Mary said, "Lord, you are fearful and wonderful, and [. . .] those who do not know you."

. . .

Mary said, "I want to understand all things, just as they are!"

. . .

Mary said, "Of what sort is that mustard seed? Is it something from heaven or is it something from earth?"

. . .

Judas said, "You have told us this out of the mind of truth. When we pray, how should we pray?" The Lord said, "Pray in the place where there is no woman." Matthew said, "'Pray in the place where there is no woman,' he tells us, meaning 'Destroy the works of womanhood,' not because there is any other manner of birth, but because they will cease giving birth." Mary said, "They will never be obliterated."

—*The Dialogue of the Savior*

Mary, Mary, know [me],
But do not touch me
Dry the tears of your eyes,
And know that I am your master,
Only do not touch me,
For I have not yet seen my father's face

Your God was not taken away,
As you thought in your pettiness.
Your God did not die;
Rather, he mastered [death].
I am not the gardener.

I have given, I have received . . . ,
I did [not] appear to you
Until I saw your tears and grief . . . for me.

Cast this sadness away
And perform this service.
Be my messenger to these lost orphans.
Hurry, with joy, go to the eleven.
You will find them gathered on the bank of the
  Jordan.
The traitor convinced them to fish
As they did earlier,
And to lay down the nets
In which they caught people for life.

Say to them, "Arise, let us go.
Your brother calls you."
If they disregard me as a brother,
Say to them, "It is your master."
If they disregard me as master,
Say to them, "It is your Lord."
Use all your skill and knowledge
Until you bring the sheep to the shepherd.

If you see they do not respond,
Make Simon Peter come to you.
Say to him, "Remember my words,
Between me and you. Remember what I said,

Between me and you, on the Mount of Olives.
I have something to say,
I have no one to whom to say it."

Rabbi, my master, I shall carry out your instructions
With joy in my whole heart.
I shall not let my heart rest,
I shall not let my eyes sleep,
I shall not let my feet relax
Until I bring the sheep to the fold.

Glory to Mary,
Because she listened to her master,
[she has] carried out his instructions
with joy in her whole heart.
[Glory and] triumph to the soul of blessed Mary.

—*The Manichaean Psalms of Heracleides*

Simon Peter said to them, "Make Mary leave us, for females are not worthy of life." Jesus said, "I myself will lead her in order to make her male, so that she too may become a living spirit resembling you males. For every female who makes herself male will enter the kingdom of Heaven."

—*The Gospel of Thomas*

SIX

Jesus's Teachings

"Lift up the stone"

For Christian Gnostics, Jesus did not bring salvation through his death and resurrection. Rather, he brought it by guiding his followers to the knowledge that had the power to redeem. Typically, therefore, Gnostic writers were less interested in the events of Jesus's life. Instead, they seek to expound the message he delivered. In the Gospel of Thomas, for example, in which there are no descriptions of events from Jesus's life, this takes the form of a series of "secret sayings" about the kingdom of God.

The primacy of knowledge is also emphasized in the Secret Book of James—also known as the Apocryphon of James—which purports to be a collection of secret revelations made by Jesus to James after his death. This book, discovered in Nag Hammadi, was probably written in the second century, though some theologians believe it may contain earlier sayings.

In the Book of St. Thomas the Contender, a second- or third-century book discovered at Nag Hammadi, Jesus speaks to his brother Thomas of "hidden things." He tells him that whoever knows oneself, understands everything. In this book Jesus imparts another Gnostic teaching: that the pure, spiritual world and the corrupt, physical world are divided. He speaks of redemption in terms of an escape from "the bitterness of this life."

Gnostics often described God in both male and female terms. In the Secret Book of John, Jesus describes himself as father, mother, and son, while in the Gospel of Philip, the Holy Spirit is cast as a female.

In a series of visions given by Jesus to Peter in the Apocalypse of Peter, a Gnostic text found in Nag Hammadi thought to date from the third century, Jesus warns of heretics and false teachers. Among them, he includes bishops and teachers who expound the orthodox belief that Jesus died on the cross. This belief is echoed—although less aggressively—in the Gospel of Philip, which claims that those without true knowledge misunderstand the meaning of terms like "resurrection," taking them too literally.

Though esoteric and centered on the idea that only a select few can be saved, Gnostic writers did sometimes preach the virtues of altruism. The Gospel of Truth urges its readers to be compassionate, strengthening the weak, feeding the hungry, and—a reference to gnosis—waking those who sleep.

The Acts of John, another partially Gnostic text, includes a story about Jesus teaching his disciples that appears nowhere else. On the night before his death, Jesus asks his disciples to stand in a circle, holding one another's hands, and dance, while he sings a hymn. During the dance, he explains that the point of his imminent suffering is to show them the nature of human suffering;

his disciples go away "dazed." Early Christians regularly enacted this dance. Gustav Holst set the hymn included in the text to music and called it "The Hymn of Jesus."

THESE are the secret sayings which the living Jesus spoke and which Didymus Judas Thomas wrote down.

And he said, "Whoever finds the interpretation of these sayings will not experience death."

Jesus said, "Let him who seeks continue seeking until he finds. When he finds, he will become troubled. When he becomes troubled, he will be astonished, and he will rule over the all."

Jesus said, "If those who lead you say to you, 'See, the kingdom is in the sky,' then the birds of the sky will precede you. If they say to you, 'It is in the sea,' then the fish will precede you. Rather, the kingdom is inside of you, and it is outside of you. When you come to know yourselves, then you will become known, and you will realize that it is you who are the sons of the living father. But if you will not know yourselves, you dwell in poverty and it is you who are that poverty."

Jesus said, "The man old in days will not hesitate to ask a small child seven days old about the place of life, and he will live. For many who are first will become last, and they will become one and the same."

Jesus said, "Recognize what is in your sight, and that which is hidden from you will become plain to you. For there is nothing hidden which will not become manifest."

His disciples questioned him and said to him, "Do you want us to fast? How shall we pray? Shall we give alms? What diet shall we observe?" Jesus said, "Do not tell lies, and do not do what you hate, for all things are plain in the sight of heaven. For nothing hidden will not become manifest, and nothing covered will remain without being uncovered."

. . .

Jesus said, "This heaven will pass away, and the one above it will pass away. The dead are not alive, and the living will not die. In the days when you consumed what is dead, you made it what is alive. When you come to dwell in the light, what will you do? On the day when you were one you became two. But when you become two, what will you do?"

. . .

Jesus said to his disciples, "Compare me to someone and tell me who I am like." Simon Peter said to him, "You are like a righteous angel." Matthew said to him, "You are like a wise philosopher." Thomas said to him, "Master, my mouth is wholly incapable of saying whom you are like." Jesus said, "I am not your master. Because you have drunk, you have become intoxicated from the bubbling spring which I have measured out." And he took him and withdrew and told him three things. When Thomas returned to his companions, they asked him, "What did Jesus say to you?" Thomas said to them, "If I tell you one of the things which he told me, you will pick up stones and throw them at me; a fire will come out of the stones and burn you up."

. . .

Jesus said, "I shall give you what no eye has seen and what no ear has heard and what no hand has touched and what has never occurred to the human mind."

The disciples said to Jesus, "Tell us how our end will be." Jesus said, "Have you discovered, then, the beginning, that you look for the end? For where the beginning is, there will the end be. Blessed is he who will take his place in the beginning; he will know the end and will not experience death."

Jesus said, "Blessed is he who came into being before he came into being. If you become my disciples and listen to my words, these stones will minister to you. For there are five trees for you in Paradise which remain undisturbed summer and winter and whose leaves do not fall. Whoever becomes acquainted with them will not experience death."

. . .

Jesus saw infants being suckled. He said to his disciples, "These infants being suckled are like those who enter the kingdom." They said to him, "Shall we then, as children, enter the kingdom?" Jesus said to them, "When you make the two one, and when you make the inside like the outside and the outside like the inside, and the above like the below, and when you make the male and the female one and the same, so that the male not be male nor the female female; and when you fashion eyes in the place of an eye, and a hand in place of a hand, and a foot in place of a foot, and a likeness in place of a likeness; then will you enter the kingdom."

Jesus said, "I shall choose you, one out of a thousand, and two out of ten thousand, and they shall stand as a single one."

His disciples said to him, "Show us the place where you are, since it is necessary for us to seek it." He said to them, "Whoever has ears, let him hear. There is light within a man of light, and he lights up the whole world. If he does not shine, he is darkness."

Jesus said, "Love your brother like your soul, guard him like the pupil of your eye."

Jesus said, "You see the mote in your brother's eye, but you do not see the beam in your own eye. When you cast the beam out of your own eye, then you will see clearly to cast the mote from your brother's eye."

. . .

Jesus said, "I took my place in the midst of the world, and I appeared to them in flesh. I found all of them intoxicated; I found none of them thirsty. And my soul became afflicted for the sons of men, because they are blind in their hearts and do not have sight; for empty they came into the world, and empty too they seek to leave the world. But for the moment they are intoxicated. When they shake off their wine, then they will repent."

Jesus said, "If the flesh came into being because of spirit, it is a wonder. But if spirit came into being because of the body, it is a wonder of wonders. Indeed, I am amazed at how this great wealth has made its home in this poverty."

Jesus said, "Where there are three gods, they are gods. Where there are two or one, I am with him."

. . .

Jesus said, "A city being built on a high mountain and fortified cannot fall, nor can it be hidden."

Jesus said, "Preach from your housetops that which you will hear in your ear. For no one lights a lamp and puts it under a bushel, nor does he put it in a hidden place, but rather he sets it on a lampstand so that everyone who enters and leaves will see its light."

Jesus said, "If a blind man leads a blind man, they will both fall into a pit."

. . .

His disciples said, "When will you become revealed to us and when shall we see you?" Jesus said, "When you disrobe without being ashamed and take up your garments and place them under your feet like little children and tread on them, then will you see the son of the living one, and you will not be afraid."

Jesus said, "Many times have you desired to hear these words which I am saying to you, and you have no one else to hear them from. There will be days when you will look for me and will not find me."

Jesus said, "The pharisees and the scribes have taken the keys of knowledge and hidden them. They themselves have not entered, nor have they allowed to enter those who wish to. You, however, be as wise as serpents and as innocent as doves."

. . .

Jesus said, "Become passersby."

His disciples said to him, "Who are you, that you should say these things to us?" Jesus said to them, "You do not realize who I am from what I say to you, but you have become like the Jews, for they [either] love the tree and hate its fruit [or] love the fruit and hate the tree."

. . .

Jesus said, "Among those born of women, from Adam until John the Baptist, there is no one so superior to John the Baptist that his eyes should not be lowered [before him]. Yet I have said, whichever one of you comes to be a child will be acquainted with the kingdom and will become superior to John."

. . .

Jesus said, "Blessed are the solitary and elect, for you will find the kingdom. For you are from it, and to it you will return."

Jesus said, "If they say to you, 'Where did you come from?,' say to them, 'We came from the light, the place where the light came into being on its own accord and established itself and became manifest through their image.' If they say to you, 'Is it you?,' say, 'We are its children, we are the elect of the living father.' If they ask you, 'What is the sign of your father in you?,' say to them, 'It is movement and repose.'"

His disciples said to him, "When will the repose of the dead come about, and when will the new world come?" He said to them, "What you look forward to has already come, but you do not recognize it."

His disciples said to him, "Twenty-four prophets spoke in Israel, and all of them spoke in you." He said to them, "You have omitted the one living in your presence and have spoken [only] of the dead."

. . .

Jesus said, "Whoever has come to understand the world has found [only] a corpse, and whoever has found a corpse is superior to the world."

. . .

Jesus said, "It is to those who are worthy of my mysteries that I tell my mysteries. Do not let your left [hand] know what your right [hand] is doing."

. . .

Jesus said, "That which you have will save you if you bring it forth from yourselves. That which you do not have within you will kill you if you do not have it within you."

. . .

Jesus said, "Many are standing at the door, but it is the solitary who will enter the bridal chamber."

. . .

Jesus said, "It is I who am the light which is above them all. It is I who am the all. From me did the all come forth, and unto me did the all extend. Split a piece of wood, and I am there. Lift up the stone, and you will find me there."

Jesus said, "Why have you come out into the desert? To see a reed shaken by the wind? And to see a man clothed in fine garments like your kings and your great men? Upon them are the fine garments, and they are unable to discern the truth."

. . .

Jesus said, "The images are manifest to man, but the light in them remains concealed in the image of the light of the father. He will become manifest, but his image will remain concealed by his light."

. . .

They said to him, "Tell us who you are so that we may believe in you." He said to them, "You read the face of the sky and of the earth, but you have not recognized the one who is before you, and you do not know how to read this moment."

Jesus said, "Seek and you will find. Yet, what you asked me about in former times and which I did not tell you then, now I do desire to tell, but you do not inquire after it."

. . .

Jesus said, "He who seeks will find, and he who knocks will be let in."

. . .

Jesus said, "When you make the two one, you will become the sons of man, and when you say, 'Mountain, move away,' it will move away."

. . .

Jesus said, "He who will drink from my mouth will become like me. I myself shall become he, and the things that are hidden will be revealed to him."

Jesus said, "The kingdom is like a man who had a hidden treasure in his field without knowing it. And after he died, he left it to his son. The son did not know [about the treasure]. He inherited the field and sold it. And the one who bought it went plowing and found the treasure. He began to lend money at interest to whomever he wished."

Jesus said, "Whoever finds the world and becomes rich, let him renounce the world."

Jesus said, "The heavens and the earth will be rolled up in your presence. And the one who lives from the living one will not see death." Does not Jesus say, "Whoever finds himself is superior to the world"?

Jesus said, "Woe to the flesh that depends on the soul; woe to the soul that depends on the flesh."

His disciples said to him, "When will the kingdom come?" Jesus said, "It will not come by waiting for it. It will not be a matter of saying 'here it is' or 'there it is.' Rather, the kingdom of the father is spread out upon the earth, and men do not see it."

—*The Gospel of Thomas*

Hearken to the word; understand knowledge; love life, and no one will persecute you, nor will anyone oppress you, other than you yourselves.

—*The Secret Book of James*

The Nazarene is he who reveals what is hidden. Christ has everything in himself—man, angel, mystery, and the Father.

—*The Gospel of Philip*

The Savior said, "Brother Thomas, while you have time in the world, listen to me, and I will reveal to you the things you have pondered in your mind.

"Now, since it has been said that you are my twin and true companion, examine yourself, and learn who you are, in what way you exist, and how you will come to be. Since you will be called my brother, it is not fitting that you be ignorant of yourself. And I know that you have understood, because you had already understood that I am the knowledge of the truth. So while you accompany me, although you are uncomprehending, you have [in fact] already come to know, and you will be called 'the one who knows himself.' For he who has not known himself has known nothing, but he who has known himself has at the same time already achieved knowledge about the depth of the all. So then, you, my brother Thomas, have beheld what is obscure to men, that is, what they ignorantly stumble against."

Now Thomas said to the Lord, "Therefore I beg you to tell me what I ask you before your ascension, and when I hear from you about the hidden things, then I can speak about them. And it is obvious to me that the truth is difficult to perform before men."

The Savior answered, saying, "If the things that are visible to you are obscure to you, how can you hear about the things that are not visible? If the deeds of the truth that are visible in the world are difficult for you to perform, how indeed, then, shall you perform those that pertain to the exalted height and to the pleroma which are not visible? And how shall you be called 'laborers'? In this respect you are apprentices, and have not yet achieved the height of perfection."

Now Thomas answered and said to the Savior, "Tell us about these things that you say are not visible, but are hidden from us."

The Savior said, "All bodies [. . .] the beasts are begotten [. . .] it is evident like [. . .] this, too, those that are above [. . .] things that are visible, but they are visible in their own root, and it is their fruit that nourishes them. But these visible bodies survive by devouring creatures similar to them with the result that the bodies change. Now that which changes will decay and perish, and has no hope of life from then on, since that body is bestial. So just as the body of the beasts perishes, so also will these formations perish. Do they not derive from intercourse like that of the beasts? If it, too, derives from intercourse, how will it beget anything different from beasts? So, therefore, you are babes until you become perfect."

And Thomas answered, "Therefore I say to you, Lord, that those who speak about things that are invisible and difficult to explain are like those who shoot their arrows at a target at night. To be sure, they shoot their arrows as anyone would—since they shoot at the target—but it is not visible. Yet when the light comes forth and hides the darkness, then the work of each will appear. And you, our light, enlighten, O Lord."

Jesus said, "It is in light that light exists."

Thomas spoke, saying, "Lord, why does this visible light that shines on behalf of men rise and set?"

The Savior said, "O blessed Thomas, of course this visible light shines on your behalf—not in order that you remain here, but rather that you might come forth—and whenever all the elect abandon bestiality, then this light will withdraw up to its essence, and its essence will welcome it, since it is a good servant."

. . .

Again the Savior answered and said, "Therefore it is necessary for us to speak to you, since this is the doctrine of the perfect. If, now, you desire to become perfect, you shall observe these things; if not, your name is 'Ignorant,' since it is impossible for an intelligent man to dwell with a fool, for the intelligent man is perfect in all wisdom. To the fool, however, the good and bad are the same—indeed the wise man will be nourished by the truth and 'will be like a tree growing by the meandering stream'—seeing that there are some who, although having wings, rush upon the visible things, things that are far from the truth. For that which guides them, the fire, will give them an illusion of truth, and will shine on them with a perishable beauty, and it will imprison them in a dark sweetness and captivate them with fragrant pleasure. And it will blind them with insatiable lust and burn their souls and become for them like a stake stuck in their heart which they can never dislodge. And like a bit in the mouth, it leads them according to its own desire. And it has fettered them with its chains and bound all their limbs with the bitterness of the bondage of lust for those visible things that will decay and change and swerve by impulse. They have always been attracted downward; as they are killed, they are assimilated to all the beasts of the perishable realm."

Thomas answered and said, "It is obvious and has been said, 'Many are [. . .] those who do not know [. . .] soul.'"

And the Savior answered, saying, "Blessed is the wise man who sought after the truth, and when he found it, he rested upon it forever and was unafraid of those who wanted to disturb him."

Thomas answered and said, "Is it beneficial for us, Lord, to rest among our own?"

The Savior said, "Yes, it is useful. And it is good for you, since things visible among men will dissolve—for the vessel of their flesh will dissolve, and when it is brought to naught it will come to be among visible things, among things that are seen. And then the fire which they see gives them pain on account of love for the faith they formerly possessed. They will be gathered back to that which is visible. Moreover, those who have sight among things that are not visible, without the first love they will perish in the concern for this life and the scorching of the fire. Only a little while longer, and that which is visible will dissolve; then shapeless shades will emerge, and in the midst of tombs they will forever dwell upon the corpses in pain and corruption of soul."

. . .

"Watch and pray that you not come to be in the flesh, but rather that you come forth from the bondage of the bitterness of this life. And as you pray, you will find rest, for you have left behind the suffering and the disgrace. For when you come forth from the sufferings and passions of the body, you will receive rest from the good one, and you will reign with the king, you joined with him and he with you, from now on, for ever and ever, Amen."

—*The Book of St. Thomas the Contender*

He said to me, "John, John, why do you doubt, or why are you afraid? You are not unfamiliar with this image, are you?—that is, do not be timid!—I am the one who is with you always. I am the Father, I am the Mother, I am the Son."

—*The Secret Book of John*

The rulers thought that it was by their own power and will that they were doing what they did, but the Holy Spirit in secret was accomplishing everything by them as it wished. Truth, which existed from the beginning, is sown everywhere. And many see it being sown, but few are they who see it being reaped.

Some say, "Mary conceived by the Holy Spirit. They do not know what they are saying. When did a woman ever conceive by a woman?"

. . .

When Eve was still with Adam, death did not exist. When she was separated from him, death came into being. If he enters again and attains his former self, death will be no more.

—*The Gospel of Philip*

As the Savior was sitting in the temple in the three hundredth (year) of the covenant and the agreement of the tenth pillar, and being satisfied with the number of the living, incorruptible Majesty, he said to me, "Peter, blessed are those above belonging to the Father, who revealed life to those who are from the life, through me, since I reminded they who are built on what is strong, that they may hear my word, and distinguish words of unrighteousness and transgression of law from righteousness, as being from the height of every word of this pleroma of truth, having been enlightened in good pleasure by him whom the principalities sought. But they did not find him, nor was he mentioned among any generation of the prophets. He has now appeared among these, in him who appeared, who is the Son of Man, who is exalted above the heavens in a fear of men of like essence. But you yourself, Peter, become perfect in accordance with your name with myself, the one who chose you, because from you I have established a base for the remnant whom I have summoned to knowledge. Therefore be strong until the imitation of righteousness—of him who had summoned you, having summoned you to know him in a way which is worth doing because of the rejection which happened to him, and the sinews of his hands and his feet, and the crowning by those of the middle region, and the body of his radiance which they bring in hope of service because of a reward of honor—as he was about to reprove you three times in this night."

And as he was saying these things, I saw the priests and the people running up to us with stones, as if they would kill us; and I was afraid that we were going to die.

And he said to me, "Peter, I have told you many times that they are blind ones who have no guide. If you want to know their blindness, put your hands upon [your] eyes—your robe—and say what you see."

But when I had done it, I did not see anything. I said, "No one sees [this way]."

Again he told me, "Do it again."

And there came in me fear with joy, for I saw a new light greater than the light of day. Then it came down upon the Savior. And I told him about those things which I saw.

And he said to me again, "Lift up your hands and listen to what the priests and the people are saying."

And I listened to the priests as they sat with the scribes. The multitudes were shouting with their voice.

When he heard these things from me he said to me, "Prick up your ears and listen to the things they are saying."

And I listened again, "As you sit, they are praising you."

And when I said these things, the Savior said, "I have told you that these [people] are blind and deaf. Now then, listen to the things which they are telling you in a mystery, and guard them. Do not tell them to the sons of this age. For they shall blaspheme you in these ages since they are ignorant of you, but they will praise you in knowledge.

"For many will accept our teaching in the beginning. And they will turn from it again by the will of the Father of their error, because they have done what he wanted. And he will reveal them in his judgment, i.e., the servants of the Word. But those who became mingled with these shall become their prisoners, since they are without perception. And the guileless, good, pure one they push to the worker of death, and to the kingdom of those who praise Christ in a restoration. And they praise the men of the propagation of falsehood, those who will come after you. And they will cleave to the name of a dead man, thinking that they will become pure. But they will become greatly defiled and they will fall into a name of error, and into the hand of an evil, cunning man and a manifold dogma, and they will be ruled without law.

"For some of them will blaspheme the truth and proclaim evil teaching. And they will say evil things against each other. Some will be named: [those] who stand in [the] strength of the archons, of a man and a naked woman who is manifold and subject to much suffering. And those who say these things will ask about dreams. And if they say that a dream came from a demon worthy of their error, then they shall be given perdition instead of incorruption.

"For evil cannot produce good fruit. For the place from which each of them is produces that which is like itself; for not every soul is of the truth, nor of immortality. For every soul of these ages has death assigned to it in our view, because it is always a slave, since it is created for its desires and their eternal destruction, in which they are and from which they are. They love the creatures of the matter which came forth with them.

"But the immortal souls are not like these, O Peter. But indeed, as long as the hour is not yet come, it [the immortal soul] shall resemble a mortal one. But it shall not reveal its nature, that it alone is the immortal one, and thinks about immortality, having faith, and desiring to renounce these things.

"For people do not gather figs from thorns or from thorn trees, if they are wise, nor grapes from thistles. For, on the one hand, that which is always becoming is in that from which it is, being from what is not good, which becomes destruction for it and death. But that which comes to be in the Eternal One is in the One of the life and the immortality of the life which they resemble.

"Therefore all that which exists not will dissolve into what exists not. For deaf and blind ones join only with their own kind.

"But others shall change from evil words and misleading mysteries. Some who do not understand mystery speak of things which they do not understand, but they will boast that the mystery of the truth is theirs alone. And in haughtiness they shall grasp at pride, to envy the immortal soul which has become a pledge. For every authority, rule, and power of the aeons wishes to be with these in the creation of the world, in order that those who are not, having been forgotten by those that are, may praise them, though they have not been saved, nor have they been brought to the Way by them, always wishing that they may become imperishable ones. For if the immortal soul receives power in an intellectual spirit—but immediately they join with one of those who misled them.

"But many others, who oppose the truth and are the messengers of error, will set up their error and their law against these pure thoughts of mine, as looking out from one [perspective] thinking that good and evil are from one [source]. They do business in my word. And they will propagate harsh fate. The race of immortal souls will go in it in vain, until my Parousia. For they shall come out of them—and my forgiveness of their transgressions, into which they fell through their adversaries, whose ransom I got from the slavery in which they were, to give them freedom that they may create an imitation remnant in the name of a dead man, who is Hermas, of the first-born of unrighteousness, in order that the light which exists may not be believed by the little ones. But those of this sort are the workers who will be cast into the outer darkness, away from the sons of light. For neither will they enter, nor do they permit those who are going up to their approval for their release.

"And still others of them who suffer think that they will perfect the wisdom of the brotherhood which really exists, which is the spiritual fellowship of those united in communion, through which the wedding of incorruptibility shall be revealed. The kindred race of the sisterhood will appear as an imitation. These are the ones who oppress their brothers, saying to them, 'Through this our God has pity, since salvation comes to us through this,' not knowing the punishment of those who are made glad by those who have done this thing to the little ones whom they saw, [and] whom they took prisoner.

"And there shall be others of those who are outside our number who name themselves bishop and also deacons, as if they have received their authority from God. They bend themselves under the judgment of the leaders. Those people are dry canals."

—*The Apocalypse of Peter*

Christ came to ransom some, to save others, to redeem others. He ransomed those who were strangers and made them his own. And he set his own apart, those whom he gave as a pledge according to his plan. It was not only when he appeared that he voluntarily laid down his life, but he voluntarily laid down his life from the very day the world came into being. Then he came first in order to take it, since it had been given as a pledge. It fell into the hands of robbers and was taken captive, but he saved it. He redeemed the good people in the world as well as the evil.

Light and Darkness, life and death, right and left, are brothers of one another. They are inseparable. Because of this neither are the good good, nor evil evil, nor is life life, nor death death. For this reason each one will dissolve into its earliest origin. But those who are exalted above the world are indissoluble, eternal.

Names given to the worldly are very deceptive, for they divert our thoughts from what is correct to what is incorrect. Thus one who hears the word "God" does not perceive what is correct, but perceives what is incorrect. So also with "the Father" and "the Son" and "the Holy Spirit" and "life" and "light" and "resurrection" and "the Church [Ekklesia]" and all the rest—people do not perceive what is correct but they perceive what is incorrect, unless they have come to know what is correct. The names which are heard are in the world [. . .] deceive. If they were in the Aeon, they would at no time be used as names in the world. Nor were they set among worldly things. They have an end in the Aeon.

—*The Gospel of Philip*

Say, then, from the heart, that you are the perfect day, and in you dwells the light that does not fail. Speak of the truth with those who search for it, and [of] knowledge to those who have committed sin in their error. Make firm the foot of those who have stumbled, and stretch out your hands to those who are ill. Feed those who are hungry, and give repose to those who are weary, and raise up those who wish to rise, and awaken those who sleep. For you are the understanding that is drawn forth. If strength acts thus, it becomes even stronger. Be concerned with yourselves; do not be concerned with other things which you have rejected from yourselves. Do not return to what you have vomited, to eat it. Do not be moths. Do not be worms, for you have already cast it off. Do not become a [dwelling] place for the devil, for you have already destroyed him. Do not strengthen [those who are] obstacles to you, who are collapsing, as though [you were] a support [for them]. For the lawless one is someone to treat ill, rather than the just one. For the former does his work as a lawless person; the latter as a righteous person does his work among others. So you, do the will of the Father, for you are from him.

—*The Gospel of Truth*

Bartholomew saith unto him: "Declare unto us, Lord, what sin is heavier than all sins?" Jesus saith unto him: "Verily I say unto thee that hypocrisy and backbiting is heavier than all sins: for because of them, the prophet said in the psalm, that 'the ungodly shall not rise in the judgment, neither sinners in the council of the righteous,' neither the ungodly in the judgment of my Father."

—*The Questions of Bartholomew*

Now before he was taken by the lawless Jews, who also were governed by [had their law from] the lawless serpent, he gathered all of us together and said: "Before I am delivered up unto them let us sing a hymn to the Father, and so go forth to that which lieth before us." He bade us therefore make as it were a ring, holding one another's hands, and himself standing in the midst he said: "Answer Amen unto me." He began, then, to sing a hymn and to say:

"Glory be to thee, Father."

And we, going about in a ring, answered him: "Amen."

"Glory be to thee, Word: Glory be to thee, Grace. Amen.

"Glory be to thee, Spirit: Glory be to thee, Holy One.

"Glory be to thy glory. Amen.

"We praise thee, O Father; we give thanks to thee, O Light, wherein darkness dwelleth not. Amen.

"Now whereas [or wherefore] we give thanks,

I say:

"I would be saved, and I would save. Amen.

"I would be loosed, and I would loose. Amen.

"I would be wounded, and I would wound. Amen.

"I would be born, and I would bear. Amen.

"I would eat, and I would be eaten. Amen.

"I would hear, and I would be heard. Amen.

"I would be thought, being wholly thought. Amen.

"I would be washed, and I would wash. Amen.

"Grace danceth. I would pipe; dance ye all. Amen.

"I would mourn: lament ye all. Amen.

"The number Eight singeth praise with us. Amen.

"The number Twelve danceth on high. Amen.

"The Whole on high hath part in our dancing. Amen.

"Whoso danceth not, knoweth not what cometh to pass. Amen.

"I would flee, and I would stay. Amen.

"I would adorn, and I would be adorned. Amen.

"I would be united, and I would unite. Amen.

"A house I have not, and I have houses. Amen.

"A place I have not, and I have places. Amen.

"A temple I have not, and I have temples. Amen.

"A lamp am I to thee that beholdest me. Amen.

"A mirror am I to thee that perceivest me. Amen.

"A door am I to thee that knockest at me. Amen.

"A way am I to thee a wayfarer.

"Now answer thou [or as thou respondest] unto my dancing. Behold thyself in me who speak, and seeing what I do, keep silence about my mysteries.

"Thou that dancest, perceive what I do, for thine is this passion of the manhood, which I am about to suffer. For thou couldest not at all have understood what thou sufferest if I had not been sent unto thee, as the word of the Father. Thou that sawest what I suffer sawest me as suffering, and seeing it thou didst not abide but wert wholly moved, moved to make wise. Thou hast me as a bed, rest upon me. Who I am, thou shalt know when I depart. What now I am seen to be, that I am not. Thou shalt see when thou comest. If thou hadst known how to suffer, thou wouldest have been able not to suffer. Learn thou to suffer, and thou shalt be able not to suffer. What thou knowest not, I myself will teach thee. Thy God am I, not the God of the traitor. I would keep tune with holy souls. In me know thou the word of wisdom. Again with me say thou: Glory be to thee, Father; glory to thee, Word; glory to thee, Holy Ghost. And if thou wouldst know concerning me, what I was, know that with a word did I deceive all things and I was no whit deceived. I have leaped: but do thou understand the whole, and having understood it, say: Glory be to thee, Father. Amen."

Thus, my beloved, having danced with us the Lord went forth. And we as men gone astray or dazed with sleep fled this way and that.

—*The Acts of John*

SEVEN

Jesus's Death

"A cross of light"

"And about the ninth hour Jesus cried with a loud voice, saying, 'Eli, Eli, lama sabachthani?' That is to say, 'My God, my God, why hast thou forsaken me?'" Thus the biblical gospel of Matthew describes Jesus's agony, and imminent death, on the cross. Anticipating this torment, in the Garden of Gethsemane a few hours earlier, Jesus is described in the gospel as "very sorrowful and heavy" and wanting the comfort of his disciples around him. As the Son of God, Jesus could foresee the agony that he had chosen to endure; yet as a man he dreaded it.

For some Gnostics, Jesus's death was neither necessary nor desirable: Jesus saved men through the knowledge he brought them, not by suffering and dying like one of them. Indeed, because some Gnostics believed that all matter was corrupt, and that Jesus was divine, they concluded that Jesus was not human, even if he looked it. Nor could he have died on the cross.

In the Apocalypse of Peter, to emphasize this belief, Jesus is described laughing while his fleshly body hangs on the tree: for the real, divine Jesus was not being crucified. In the Acts of John, Jesus appears in a cave on the Mount of Olives at the same time as his human guise is being crucified. He reassures John, telling him that his death is "contrived . . . symbolically." In the First Apocalypse of James, Jesus again comforts one of his followers, telling him he did not suffer during his supposed crucifixion.

The Gospel of Philip says that Jesus cried out to ask God why he had "forsaken" him at the moment that he "departed from that place." The suggestion that the divine Jesus abandoned his borrowed body on the cross was perhaps inspired by a belief among some Gnostics that he had entered it at baptism.

The Second Treatise of the Great Seth contends that someone else took Jesus's place on the cross. The writer is scornful of those who preach "the doctrine of a dead man." But some Gnostic books treat the crucifixion with more deference. The author of the Gospel of Truth suggests that Jesus on the cross should be regarded as "fruit on the tree"—the tree of knowledge in Paradise.

There are also two interesting accounts of the crucifixion in two non-Gnostic, yet noncanonical, texts. The Gospel of Nicodemus, which may be from the fifth century, is solely about Jesus's death and resurrection. Fiercely anti-Semitic, it attempts to vindicate Pontius Pilate for his role in Jesus's death. It was often used as a basis for medieval religious dramas, and also gives a name to a woman who in the Bible is anonymous but later became a popular figure, with her own Station of the Cross: Veronica.

The Gospel of Peter, which is thought to date from the early second century, or even earlier, also gives a detailed description of Jesus's trial, death, and resurrection. It is the earliest noncanonical account of Jesus's passion. Like the Gospel of Nicodemus, this book condemns the Jews for Jesus's death, though it strikes a docetic note in suggesting that Jesus did not suffer on the cross. That may be why it was banned by the early Church, having been popular in the second century. It subsequently fell out of use, and a fragment of it was discovered, on an eighth- or ninth-century manuscript, in Egypt in 1886.

WHEN he said those things, I saw him seemingly being seized by them. And I said, "What do I see, O Lord, that it is you yourself whom they take, and that you are grasping me? Or who is this one, glad and laughing on the tree? And is it another one whose feet and hands they are striking?"

The Savior said to me, "He whom you saw on the tree, glad and laughing, this is the living Jesus. But this one into whose hands and feet they drive the nails is his fleshly part, which is the substitute being put to shame, the one who came into being in his likeness. But look at him and me."

But I, when I had looked, said, "Lord, no one is looking at you. Let us flee this place."

But he said to me, "I have told you, 'Leave the blind alone!' And you, see how they do not know what they are saying. For the son of their glory instead of my servant, they have put to shame."

And I saw someone about to approach us resembling him, even him who was laughing on the tree. And he was filled with a Holy Spirit, and he is the Savior. And there was a great, ineffable light around them, and the multitude of ineffable and invisible angels blessing them. And when I looked at him, the one who gives praise was revealed.

And he said to me, "Be strong, for you are the one to whom these mysteries have been given, to know them through revelation, that he whom they crucified is the first-born, and the home of demons, and the stony vessel, in which they dwell, of Elohim, of the cross, which is under the Law. But he who stands near him is the living Savior, the first in him, whom they seized and released, who stands joyfully looking at those who did him violence, while they are divided among themselves. Therefore he laughs at their lack of perception, knowing that they are born blind. So then the one susceptible to suffering shall come, since the body is the substitute. But what they released was my incorporeal body. But I am the intellectual Spirit filled with radiant light. He whom you saw coming to me is our intellectual pleroma, which unites the perfect light with my Holy Spirit."

—*The Apocalypse of Peter*

I, then, when I saw him suffer, did not even abide by his suffering, but fled unto the Mount of Olives, weeping at that which had befallen. And when he was crucified on the Friday, at the sixth hour of the day, darkness came upon all the earth. And my Lord standing in the midst of the cave and enlightening it, said: "John, unto the multitude below in Jerusalem I am being crucified and pierced with lances and reeds, and gall and vinegar is given me to drink. But unto thee I speak, and what I speak hear thou. I put it into thy mind to come up into this mountain, that thou mightest hear those things which it behoveth a disciple to learn from his teacher and a man from his God."

And having thus spoken, he showed me a cross of light fixed [set up], and about the cross a great multitude, not having one form: and in it [the cross] was one form and one likeness. And the Lord himself I beheld above the cross, not having any shape, but only a voice: and a voice not such as was familiar to us, but one sweet and kind and truly of God, saying unto me: "John, it is needful that one should hear these things from me, for I have need of one that will hear. This cross of light is sometimes called the [or a] word by me for your sakes, sometimes mind, sometimes Jesus, sometimes Christ, sometimes door, sometimes a way, sometimes bread, sometimes seed, sometimes resurrection, sometimes Son, sometimes Father, sometimes

Spirit, sometimes life, sometimes truth, sometimes faith, sometimes grace. And by these names it is called as toward men: but that which it is in truth, as conceived of in itself and as spoken of unto you, it is the marking-off of all things, and the firm uplifting of things fixed out of things unstable, and the harmony of wisdom, and indeed wisdom in harmony. There are places of the right hand and the left, powers also, authorities, lordships and demons, workings, threatenings, wraths, devils, Satan, and the lower root whence the nature of the things that come into being proceeded.

"This cross, then, is that which fixed all things apart by the word, and separated off the things that are from those that are below, and then also, being one, streamed forth into all things. But this is not the cross of wood which thou wilt see when thou goest down hence: neither am I he that is on the cross, whom now thou seest not, but only hearest his voice. I was reckoned to be that which I am not, not being what I was unto many others: but they will call me something else which is vile and not worthy of me. As, then, the place of rest is neither seen nor spoken of, much more shall I, the Lord thereof, be neither seen nor spoken of.

"Now the multitude of one aspect that is about the cross is the lower nature: and they whom thou seest in the cross, if they have not one form, it is because not yet hath every member of him that came down been comprehended. But when the human nature is taken up, and the race which draweth near unto me and obeyeth my voice, he that now heareth me shall be united therewith, and shall no more be that which now he is, but above them, as I also now am. For so long as thou callest not thyself mine, I am not that which I am: but if thou hear me, thou, hearing, shall be as I am, and I shall be that which I was, when I thee as I am with myself. For from me thou art that. Care not therefore for the many, and them that are outside the mystery despise; for know thou that I am wholly with the Father, and the Father with me.

"Nothing, therefore, of the things which they will say of me have I suffered: nay, that suffering also which I showed unto thee and the rest in the dance, I will that it be called a mystery. For what thou art, thou seest, for I showed it thee; but what I am I alone know, and no man else. Suffer me then to keep that which is mine, and that which is thine behold thou through me, and behold me in truth, that I am, not what I said, but what thou art able to know, because thou art akin thereto. Thou hearest that I suffered, yet did I not suffer; that I suffered not, yet did I suffer; that I was pierced, yet I was not smitten; hanged, and I was not hanged; that blood flowed from me, and it flowed not; and, in a word, what they say of me, that befell me not, but what they say not, that did I suffer. Now what those things are I signify unto thee, for I know that thou wilt understand. Perceive thou therefore in me the praising of the Word, the piercing of the Word, the blood of the Word, the wound of the Word, the hanging up of the Word, the suffering of the Word, the nailing of the Word, the death of the Word. And so speak I, separating off the manhood. Perceive thou therefore in the first place of the Word; then shalt thou perceive the Lord, and in the third place the man, and what he hath suffered."

When he had spoken unto me these things, and others which I know not how to say as he would have me, he was taken up, no one of the multitudes having beheld him. And when I went down I laughed them all to scorn, inasmuch as he had told me the things which they have said concerning him; holding fast this one thing in myself, that the Lord contrived all things symbolically and by a dispensation toward men, for their conversion and salvation.

—*The Acts of John*

James said, "Rabbi, how, after these things, will you appear to us again? After they seize you, and you complete this destiny, you will go up to Him-who-is." The Lord said, "James, after these things I shall reveal to you everything, not for your sake alone but for the sake of the unbelief of men, so that faith may exist in them . . . And after this I shall appear to reproof to the archons. And I shall reveal to them that he cannot be seized. If they seize him, then he will overpower each one of them. But now I shall go. Remember the things that I have spoken and let them go up before you." James said, "Lord, I shall hasten as you have said." The Lord said farewell to him and fulfilled what was fitting.

When James heard of his suffering and was much distressed, they awaited again the sign of his coming. And he came after several days . . . And the Lord appeared to him. Then he stopped his prayer and embraced him. He kissed him, saying, "Rabbi, I have found you! I have heard of your sufferings, which you endured. And I have been much distressed. My compassion you know. Therefore, on reflection, I was wishing that I would not see this people. They must be judged for these things that they have done. For these things they have done are contrary to what is fitting."

The Lord said, "James, do not be concerned for me or for this people. I am he who was within me. Never have I suffered in any way, not have I been distressed. And this people has done me no harm."

—*The First Apocalypse of James*

And I was in the mouths of lions. And the plan which they devised about me to release their Error and their senselessness—I did not succumb to them as they had planned. But I was not afflicted at all. Those who were there punished me. And I did not die in reality but in appearance, lest I be put to shame by them because these are my kinsfolk. I removed the shame from me and I did not become fainthearted in the face of what happened to me at their hands. I was about to succumb to fear, and I [suffered] according to their sight and thought, in order that they may never find any word to speak about them. For my death, which they think happened, [happened] to them in their error and blindness, since they nailed their man unto their death. For their Ennoias did not see me, for they were deaf and blind. But in doing these things, they condemn themselves. Yes, they saw me; they punished me. It was another, their father, who drank the gall and the vinegar; it was not I. They struck me with the reed; it was another, Simon, who bore the cross on his shoulder. I was another upon whom they placed the crown of thorns. But I was rejoicing in the height over all the wealth of the archons and the offspring of their error, of their empty glory. And I was laughing at their ignorance.

And I subjected all their powers. For as I came downward, no one saw me. For I was altering my shapes, changing from form to form. And therefore, when I was at their gates, I assumed their likeness. For I passed them by quietly, and I was viewing the places, and I was not afraid nor ashamed, for I was undefiled. And I was speaking with them, mingling with them through those who are mine, and trampling on those who are harsh to them with zeal, and quenching the flame. And I was doing all these things because of my desire to accomplish what I desired by the will of the Father above.

. . .

They nailed him to the tree, and they fixed him with four nails of brass. The veil of his temple he tore with his hands. It was a trembling which seized the chaos of the earth, for the souls which were in the sleep below were released. And they arose. They went about boldly, having shed zealous service of ignorance and unlearnedness beside the dead tombs, having put on the new man, since they have come to know that perfect Blessed One of the eternal and incomprehensible Father and the infinite light, which is I, since I came to my own and united them with myself.

. . .

For it was ludicrous. It is I who bear witness that it was ludicrous, since the archons do not know that it is an ineffable union of undefiled truth, as exists among the sons of light, of which they made an imitation, having proclaimed a doctrine of a dead man and lies so as to resemble the freedom and purity of the perfect assembly, [joining] themselves with their doctrine to fear and slavery, worldly cares, and abandoned worship, being small, ignorant, since they do not contain the nobility of truth, for they hate the one in whom they are, and love the one in whom they are not.

—*The Second Treatise of the Great Seth*

"My God, my God, why, O Lord, have you forsaken me?" It was on the cross that he said these words, for he had departed from that place.

. . .

Philip the apostle said, "Joseph the carpenter planted a garden because he needed wood for his trade. It was he who made the cross from the trees which he planted. His own offspring hung on that which he planted. His offspring was Jesus and the planting was the cross."

—*The Gospel of Philip*

Through this, the gospel of the one who is searched for, which [was] revealed to those who are perfect, through the mercies of the Father, the hidden mystery, Jesus, the Christ, enlightened those who were in darkness through oblivion. He enlightened them; he showed [them] a way; and the way is the truth which he taught them.

For this reason, error grew angry at him, persecuted him, was distressed at him, [and] was brought to naught. He was nailed to a tree [and] he became fruit of the knowledge of the Father. It did not, however, cause destruction because it was eaten, but to those who ate it, it gave [cause] to become glad in the discovery, and he discovered them in himself, and they discovered him in themselves.

—*The Gospel of Truth*

For the chief priests and scribes assembled in council, even Annas and Caiaphas and Somne and Dothaim and Gamaliel, Judas, Levi and Nepthalim, Alexander and Jairus and the rest of the Jews, and came unto Pilate accusing Jesus for many deeds, saying: "We know this man, that he is the son of Joseph the carpenter, begotten of Mary, and he saith that he is the Son of God and a king; moreover he doth pollute the Sabbaths and he would destroy the law of our fathers."

. . .

And Pilate called the messenger and said unto him: "Let Jesus be brought hither, but with gentleness."

. . .

Now one of the Jews came forward and besought the governor that he might speak a word. The governor saith: "If thou wilt say aught, speak on." And the Jew said: "Thirty and eight years lay I on a bed in suffering of pains, and at the coming of Jesus many that were possessed and laid with divers diseases were healed by him, and certain [faithful] young men took pity on me and carried me with my bed and brought me unto him; and when Jesus saw me he had compassion, and spake a word unto me: 'Take up thy bed and walk.' And I took up my bed and walked." The Jews say unto Pilate: "Ask of him what day it was whereon he was healed?" He that was healed saith: "On the Sabbath." The Jews say: "Did we not inform thee so, that upon the Sabbath he healeth and casteth out devils?"

And another Jew came forward and said: "I was born blind: I heard words but I saw no man's face: and as Jesus passed by I cried with a loud voice: 'Have mercy on me, O son of David.' And he took pity on me and put his hands upon mine eyes and I received sight immediately." And another Jew came forward and said: "I was bowed and he made me straight with a word." And another said: "I was a leper, and he healed me with a word."

And a certain woman named Veronica crying out from afar off said: "I had an issue of blood and touched the hem of his garment, and the flowing of my blood was stayed which I had twelve years."

—*The Gospel of Nicodemus*

But of the Jews no man washed his hands, neither did Herod nor any one of his judges: and whereas they would not wash, Pilate rose up. And then

Herod the king commanded that the Lord should be taken into their hands, saying unto them: "All that I commanded you to do unto him, do ye."

Now there stood there Joseph the friend of Pilate and of the Lord, and he, knowing that they were about to crucify him, came unto Pilate and begged the body of Jesus for burial. And Pilate sending unto Herod, begged his body. And Herod said: "Brother Pilate, even if none had begged for him, we should have buried him, since also the Sabbath dawneth; for it is written in the law that the sun should not set upon one that hath been slain [murdered]."

And he delivered him unto the people before the first day of unleavened bread, even their feast. And they having taken the Lord pushed him as they ran, and said: "Let us hail the Son of God, now that we have authority over him." And they put on him a purple robe, and made him sit upon the seat of judgment, saying: "Give righteous judgment, thou King of Israel." And one of them brought a crown of thorns and set it upon the Lord's head; and others stood and did spit in his eyes, and others buffeted his cheeks; and others did prick him with a reed, and some of them scourged him, saying. "With this honor let us honor the son of God."

And they brought two malefactors, and crucified the Lord between them. But he kept silence, as one feeling no pain. And when they set the cross upright, they wrote thereon: This is the King of Israel. And they laid his garments before him, and divided them among themselves and cast the lot upon them. But one of those malefactors reproached them, saying: "We have thus suffered for the evils which we have done; but this man which hath become the Savior of men, wherein hath he injured you?" And they were wroth with him, and commanded that his legs should not be broken, that so he might die in torment.

Now it was noonday, and darkness prevailed over all Judaea: and they were troubled and in an agony lest the sun should have set, for that he yet lived: for it is written for them that the sun should not set upon him that hath been slain (murdered). And one of them said: "Give ye him to drink gall with vinegar": and they mingled it and gave him to drink: and they fulfilled all things and accomplished their sins upon their own heads. And many went about with lamps, supposing that it was night: and some fell. And the Lord cried out aloud saying: "My power, my power, thou hast forsaken me." And when he had so said, he was taken up.

And in the same hour was the veil of the temple of Jerusalem rent in two.

And then they plucked the nails from the hands of the Lord and laid him upon the earth: and the whole earth was shaken, and there came a great fear on all.

Then the sun shone forth, and it was found to be the ninth hour. And the Jews rejoiced, and gave his body unto Joseph to bury it, because he had beheld all the good things which he did. And he took the Lord and washed him and wrapped him in linen and brought him unto his own sepulchre, which is called the Garden of Joseph.

Then the Jews and the elders and the priests, when they perceived how great an evil they had done themselves, began to lament and to say: "Woe unto our sins: the judgment and the end of Jerusalem is drawn nigh."

But I with my fellows was in grief, and we were wounded in our minds and would have hid ourselves; for we were sought after by them as malefactors, and as thinking to set the temple on fire. And beside all these things we were fasting, and we sat mourning and weeping night and day until the Sabbath.

—*The Gospel of Peter*

EIGHT

Afterward

The Risen Christ

"And if Christ be not risen, then is our preaching vain, and your faith is also vain" (1 Corinthians 15:14).

Christians' fundamental belief is that Jesus rose from the dead. But the actual event of the resurrection is not described in the Bible. The closest we get to it in early Christian literature is in the Gospel of Peter. In this book, Jesus emerges from the tomb supported by two giant angels, whose heads reach up to heaven. They are followed by a speaking cross. When a "voice from heaven" asks Jesus if he has preached to the dead, the cross replies "yea."

The Gospel of Nicodemus contains a story that was cherished by the early Church: Jesus's descent into hell. In the Bible, this is described briefly in 1 Peter, which says that, after his death, Jesus "went and preached to the spirits in prison." The Gospel of Nicodemus transforms this into a dramatic narrative. Jesus hammers at the gates of hell, overpowers Satan, and gathers up the saints and prophets of the Old Testament. Making the sign of the cross, he departs, holding Adam's right hand. The "harrowing of hell," as it later became known, was a popular subject for medieval mystery plays.

Here, as in the Bible, Jesus's appearances after his death were principally designed to convince his followers that the crucified Jesus had risen from the tomb. The Gnostic writers, of course, were less interested in this. But the resurrection did serve one useful purpose for these writers: it provided Jesus with an open-ended period of time to lead his followers to gnosis and teach them away from the wider community. Many Gnostic passages are written in the form of postresurrection dialogues.

In the Sophia of Jesus Christ, Jesus's ministry is clearly incomplete after the resurrection. Reunited with his disciples, he is asked to explain "the underlying reality of the universe and the plan."

And several Gnostic texts specifically magnify the time Jesus remained on the earth after his resurrection. In the biblical Acts of the Apostles, Jesus continues appearing to people for forty days before he ascends into heaven. In the Secret Book of James, the disciples are still having conversations with Jesus 550 days after he has risen from the dead. The Pistis Sophia, meanwhile, says he spent eleven years with his followers after the resurrection—more than four times the length of his earthly ministry as it is measured in the Bible.

The Treatise on the Resurrection is a Gnostic text that celebrates the resurrection. An anonymous teacher explains to his pupil Rheginos that the resurrection is real—but the world is an illusion.

AND early in the morning as the Sabbath dawned, there came a multitude from Jerusalem and the region roundabout to see the sepulchre that had been sealed.

Now in the night whereon the Lord's day dawned, as the soldiers were keeping guard two by two in every watch, there came a great sound in the heaven, and they saw the heavens opened and two men descend thence, shining with a great light, and drawing near unto the sepulchre. And that stone which had been set on the door rolled away of itself and went back to the side, and the sepulchre was opened and both of the young men entered in. When therefore those soldiers saw that, they waked up the centurion and the elders (for they also were there keeping watch); and while they were yet telling them the things which they had seen, they saw again three men come out of the sepulchre, and two of them sustaining the other, and a cross following, after them. And of the two they saw that their heads reached unto heaven, but of him that was led by them that it overpassed the heavens. And they heard a voice out of the heavens saying: "Hast thou preached unto them that sleep?" And an answer was heard from the cross, saying: "Yea."

Those men therefore took counsel one with another to go and report these things unto Pilate. And while they yet thought thereabout, again the heavens were opened and a man descended and entered into the tomb. And they that were with the centurion [or the centurion and they that were with him] when they saw that, hasted to go by night unto Pilate and left the sepulchre whereon they were keeping watch, and told all that they had seen, and were in great agony, saying: "Of a truth he was the son of God."

—*The Gospel of Peter*

There came certain of the guard which the Jews had asked of Pilate to keep the sepulchre of Jesus lest peradventure his disciples should come and steal him away. And they spake and declared unto the rulers of the synagogue and the priests and the Levites that which had come to pass: how that there was a great earthquake, and we saw an angel descend from heaven, and he rolled away the stone from the mouth of the cave, and sat upon it. And he did shine like snow and like lightning, and we were sore afraid and lay as dead men. And we heard the voice of the angel speaking with the women which waited at the sepulchre, saying:

"Fear ye not: for I know that ye seek Jesus which was crucified. He is not here: he is risen, as he said. Come, see the place where the Lord lay, and go quickly and say unto his disciples that he is risen from the dead, and is in Galilee."

The Jews say: "With what women spake he?" They of the guard say: "We know not who they were." The Jews say: "At what hour was it?" They of the guard say: "At midnight." The Jews say: "And wherefore did ye not take the women?" They of the guard say: "We were become as dead men through fear, and we looked not to see the light of the day; how then could we take them?" The Jews say: "As the Lord liveth, we believe you not." They of the guard say unto the Jews: "So many signs saw ye in that man, and ye believed not, how then should ye believe us? Verily ye sware rightly 'as the Lord liveth,' for he liveth indeed." Again they of the guard say: "We have heard that ye shut up him that begged the body of Jesus, and that ye scaled the door; and when ye had opened it ye found him not. Give ye therefore Joseph and we will give you Jesus." The Jews say: "Joseph is departed unto his own city." They of the guard say unto the Jews: "Jesus also is risen, as we have heard of the angel, and he is in Galilee."

. . .

Now a certain priest named Phinees and Addas a teacher and Aggaeus a Levite came down from

Galilee unto Jerusalem and told the rulers of the synagogue and the priests and the Levites, saying: "We saw Jesus and his disciples sitting upon the mountain which is called Mamilch, and he said unto his disciples: 'Go into all the world and preach unto every creature [the whole creation]: he that believeth and is baptized shall be saved, but he that disbelieveth shall be condemned. And these signs shall follow upon them that believe: in my name they shall cast out devils, they shall speak with new tongues, they shall take up serpents, and if they drink any deadly thing it shall not hurt them: they shall lay hands upon the sick and they shall recover.' And while Jesus yet spake unto his disciples we saw him taken up into heaven."

. . .

And on the morrow, which was the preparation, the rulers of the synagogue and the priests and the Levites rose up early and came to the house of Nicodemus, and Nicodemus met them and said: "Peace be unto you." And they said: "Peace be unto thee and to Joseph and unto all thy house and to all the house of Joseph." And he brought them into his house. And the whole council was set, and Joseph sat between Annas and Caiaphas and no man durst speak unto him a word. And Joseph said: "Why is it that ye have called me?" And they beckoned unto Nicodemus that he should speak unto Joseph. And Nicodemus opened his mouth and said unto Joseph: "Father, thou knowest that the reverend doctors and the priests and the Levites seek to learn a matter of thee." And Joseph said: "Inquire ye." And Annas and Caiaphas took the book of the law and adjured Joseph saying: "Give glory to the God of Israel and make confession unto him: for Achar, when he was adjured of the prophet Jesus [Joshua], foresware not himself but declared unto him all things and hid not a word from him: thou therefore also hide not from us so much as a word." And Joseph: "I will not hide one word from you." And they said unto him: "We were greatly vexed because thou didst beg the body of Jesus and wrappedst it in a clean linen cloth and didst lay him in a tomb. And for this cause we put thee in safeguard in a house wherein was no window, and we put keys and seals upon the doors, and guards did keep the place wherein thou wast shut up. And on the first day of the week we opened it and found thee not, and we were sore troubled, and amazement fell upon all the people of the Lord until yesterday. Now, therefore, declare unto us what befell thee."

And Joseph said: "On the preparation day about the tenth hour ye did shut me up, and I continued there the whole Sabbath. And at midnight as I stood and prayed the house wherein ye shut me up was taken up by the four corners, and I saw as it were a flashing of light in mine eyes, and being filled with fear I fell to the earth. And one took me by the hand and removed me from the place whereon I had fallen; and moisture of water was shed on me from my head unto my feet, and an odor of ointment came about my nostrils. And he wiped my face and kissed me and said unto me: 'Fear not, Joseph: open thine eyes and see who it is that speaketh with thee.' And I looked up and saw Jesus and I trembled, and supposed that it was a spirit: and I said the commandments: and he said them with me. And [as] ye are not ignorant that a spirit, if it meet any man and hear the commandments, straightway fleeth. And when I perceived that he said them with me, I said unto him: 'Rabbi Elias?' And he said unto me: 'I am not Elias.' And I said unto him: 'Who art thou, Lord?' And he said unto me: 'I am Jesus, whose body thou didst beg of Pilate, and didst clothe me in clean linen and cover my face with a napkin, and lay me in thy new cave and roll a great stone upon the door of the cave.' And I said to him that spake with me: 'Show me the place where I laid thee.' And he brought me and showed me the place where I laid him, and the linen cloth lay therein, and the napkin that was upon his face. And I knew that it was Jesus. And he took me by the hand and set me in the midst of mine house, the doors being shut, and laid me upon my bed and said unto me: 'Peace be unto thee.' And he kissed me and said unto me:

'Until forty days be ended go not out of thine house: for behold I go unto my brethren into Galilee.'"

And when the rulers of the synagogue and the priests and the Levites heard these words of Joseph they became as dead men and fell to the ground, and they fasted until the ninth hour. And Nicodemus with Joseph comforted Annas and Caiaphas and the priests and the Levites, saying: "Rise up and stand on your feet and taste bread and strengthen your souls, for tomorrow is the Sabbath of the Lord." And they rose up and prayed unto God and did eat and drink, and departed every man to his house.

. . .

And Joseph arose and said unto Annas and Caiaphas: "Truly and of right do ye marvel because ye have heard that Jesus hath been seen alive after death, and that he hath ascended into heaven. Nevertheless it is more marvelous that he rose not alone from the dead, but did raise up alive many other dead out of their sepulchres, and they have been seen of many in Jerusalem. And now hearken unto me; for we all know the blessed Simeon, the high priest which received the child Jesus in his hands in the temple. And this Simeon had two sons, brothers in blood and we all were at their falling asleep and at their burial. Go therefore and look upon their sepulchres: for they are open, because they have risen, and behold they are in the city of Arimathaea dwelling together in prayer. And indeed men hear them crying out, yet they speak with no man, but are silent as dead men. But come, let us go unto them and with all honor and gentleness bring them unto us, and if we adjure them, perchance they will tell us concerning the mystery of their rising again."

When they heard these things, they all rejoiced. And Annas and Caiaphas, Nicodemus and Joseph and Gamaliel went and found them not in their sepulchre, but they went unto the city of Arimathaea, and found them there, kneeling on their knees and giving themselves unto prayer. And they kissed them, and with all reverence and in the fear of God they brought them to Jerusalem into the synagogue. And they shut the doors and took the law of the Lord and put it into their hands, and adjured them by the God Adonai and the God of Israel which spake unto our fathers by the prophets, saying: "Believe ye that it is Jesus which raised you from the dead? Tell us how ye have arisen from the dead."

And when Karinus and Leucius heard this adjuration, they trembled in their body and groaned, being troubled in heart. And looking up together unto heaven they made the seal of the cross with their fingers upon their tongues, and forthwith they spake both of them, saying: "Give us each a volume of paper, and let us write that which we have seen and heard." And they gave them unto them, and each of them sat down and wrote, saying:

"O Lord Jesus Christ, the life and resurrection of the dead suffer us to speak of the mysteries of thy majesty which thou didst perform after thy death upon the cross, inasmuch as we have been adjured by thy Name. For thou didst command us thy servants to tell no man the secrets of thy divine majesty which thou wroughtest in hell.

"Now when we were set together with all our fathers in the deep, in obscurity of darkness, on a sudden there came a golden heat of the sun and a purple and royal light shining upon us. And immediately the father of the whole race of men, together with all the patriarchs and prophets, rejoiced, saying: 'This light is the beginning of everlasting light which did promise to send unto us his co-eternal light.' And Esaias cried out and said: 'This is the light of the Father, even the Son of God, according as I prophesied when I lived upon the earth.'"

. . .

And after that there came one as it were a dweller in the wilderness, and he was inquired of by all: "Who art thou?" And he answered them and said: "I am John, the voice and the prophet of the most High, which came before the face of his advent to prepare his ways, to give knowledge of salvation unto his people, for the remission of their sins. And when I saw him coming unto me, being moved of the Holy Ghost, I said: 'Behold the Lamb of God, behold him that taketh away the sins of the world.' And I baptized him in the river of Jordan, and saw the Holy Ghost descending upon him in the likeness of a dove, and heard a voice out of heaven saying: 'This is my beloved Son, in whom I am well pleased.' And now have I come before his face, and come down to declare unto you that he is at hand to visit us, even the day spring, the Son of God, coming from on high unto us that sit in darkness and in the shadow of death."

And when father Adam that was first created heard this, even that Jesus was baptized in Jordan, he cried out to Seth his son, saying: "Declare unto thy sons the patriarchs and the prophets all that thou didst hear from Michael the archangel, when I sent thee unto the gates of paradise that thou mightest entreat God to send thee his angel to give thee the oil of the tree of mercy to anoint my body when I was sick." Then Seth drew near unto the holy patriarchs and prophets, and said: "When I, Seth, was praying at the gates of paradise, behold Michael the angel of the Lord appeared unto me, saying: 'I am sent unto thee from the Lord: it is I that am set over the body of man. And I say unto thee, Seth, vex not thyself with tears, praying and entreating for the oil of the tree of mercy, that thou mayest anoint thy father Adam for the pain of his body: for thou wilt not be able to receive it save in the last days and times, save when five thousand and five hundred years are accomplished: then shall the most beloved Son of God come upon the earth to raise up the body of Adam and the bodies of the dead, and he shall come and be baptized in Jordan. And when he is come forth of the water of Jordan, then shall he anoint with the oil of mercy all that believe on him, and that oil of mercy shall be unto all generations of them that shall be born of water and of the Holy Ghost, unto life eternal. Then shall the most beloved Son of God, even Christ Jesus, come down upon the earth and shall bring in our father Adam into paradise unto the tree of mercy.'"

And when they heard all these things of Seth, all the patriarchs and prophets rejoiced with a great rejoicing.

And while all the saints were rejoicing, behold Satan the prince and chief of death said unto Hell: "Make thyself ready to receive Jesus who boasteth himself that he is the Son of God, whereas he is a man that feareth death, and sayeth: 'My soul is sorrowful even unto death.' And he hath been much mine enemy, doing me great hurt, and many that I had made blind, lame, dumb, leprous, and possessed he hath healed with a word: and some whom I have brought unto thee dead, them hath he taken away from thee."

Hell answered and said unto Satan the prince: "Who is he that is so mighty, if he be a man that feareth death? For all the mighty ones of the earth are held in subjection by my power, even they whom thou hast brought me subdued by thy power. If, then, thou art mighty, what manner of man is this Jesus who, though he fear death, resisteth thy power? If he be so mighty in his manhood, verily I say unto thee he is almighty in his god-head, and no man can withstand his power."

. . .

Hell answered and said: "Thou hast told me that it is he that hath taken away dead men from me. For there be many which while they lived on the earth have taken dead men from me, yet not by their own power but by prayer to God, and their almighty God hath taken them from me. Who is this Jesus which by his own word without prayer hath drawn dead men from me?"

. . .

And as Satan the prince, and Hell, spoke this together, suddenly there came a voice as of thunder and a spiritual cry: "Remove, O princes, your gates, and be ye lift up ye everlasting doors, and the King of glory shall come in." When Hell heard that he said unto Satan the prince: "Depart from me and go out of mine abode: if thou be a mighty man of war, fight thou against the King of glory. But what hast thou to do with him?" And Hell cast Satan forth out of his dwelling. Then said Hell unto his wicked ministers: "Shut ye the hard gates of brass and put on them the bars of iron and withstand stoutly, lest we that hold captivity be taken captive."

But when all the multitude of the saints heard it, they spake with a voice of rebuking unto Hell: "Open thy gates, that the King of glory may come in." And David cried out, saying: "Did I not when I was alive upon earth, foretell unto you: Let them give thanks unto the Lord, even his mercies and his wonders unto the children of men; who hath broken the gates of brass and smitten the bars of iron in sunder? He hath taken them out of the way of their iniquity." And thereafter in like manner Esaias said: "Did not I when I was alive upon earth foretell unto you: 'The dead shall arise, and they that are in the tombs shall rise again, and they that are in the earth shall rejoice, for the dew which cometh of the Lord is their healing'? And again I said: 'O death, where is thy sting? O Hell, where is thy victory?'"

When they heard that of Esaias, all the saints said unto Hell: "Open thy gates: now shalt thou be overcome and weak and without strength." And there came a great voice as of thunder, saying: "Remove, O princes, your gates, and be ye lift up ye doors of hell, and the King of glory shall come in." And when Hell saw that they so cried out twice, he said, as if he knew it not: "Who is the King of glory?" And David answered Hell and said: "The words of this cry do I know, for by his spirit I prophesied the same; and now I say unto thee that which I said before: The Lord strong and mighty, the Lord mighty in battle, he is the King of glory." And: "The Lord looked down from heaven that he might hear the groanings of them that are in fetters and deliver the children of them that have been slain. And now, O thou most foul and stinking Hell, open thy gates, that the King of glory may come in." And as David spake thus unto Hell, the Lord of majesty appeared in the form of a man and lightened the eternal darkness and brake the bonds that could not be loosed: and the succor of his everlasting might visited us that sat in the deep darkness of our transgressions and in the shadow of death of our sins.

When Hell and death and their wicked ministers saw that, they were stricken with fear, they and their cruel officers, at the sight of the brightness of so great light in their own realm, seeing Christ of a sudden in their abode, and they cried out, saying: "We are overcome by thee. Who art thou that art sent by the Lord for our confusion? Who art thou that without all damage of corruption, and with the signs of thy majesty unblemished, dost in wrath condemn our power? Who art thou that art so great and so small, both humble and exalted, both soldier and commander, a marvelous warrior in the shape of a bondsman, and a King of glory dead and living, whom the cross bare slain upon it? Thou that didst lie dead in the sepulchre hast come down unto us living and at thy death all creation quaked and all the stars were shaken and thou hast become free among the dead and dost rout our legions. Who art thou that settest free the prisoners that are held bound by original sin and restorest them into their former liberty?"

. . .

Then did the King of glory in his majesty trample upon death, and laid hold on Satan the prince and delivered him unto the power of Hell, and drew Adam to him unto his own brightness.

. . .

And the Lord stretching forth his hand, said: "Come unto me, all ye my saints which bear mine image and my likeness. Ye that by the tree and the devil and death were condemned, behold now the devil and death condemned by the tree." And forthwith all the saints were gathered in one under the hand of the Lord.

. . .

And the Lord stretched forth his hand and made the sign of the cross over Adam and over all his saints, and he took the right hand of Adam and went up out of hell, and all the saints followed him. . . .

—*The Gospel of Nicodemus*

After he rose from the dead, his twelve disciples and seven women continued to be his followers, and went to Galilee onto the mountain called "Divination and Joy." When they gathered together and were perplexed about the underlying reality of the universe and the plan, and the holy providence, and the power of the authorities, and about everything the Savior was doing with them in the secret of the holy plan, the Savior appeared—not in his previous form, but in the invisible spirit. And his likeness resembled a great angel of light. But his resemblance I must not describe. No mortal flesh could endure it, but only pure, perfect flesh, like that which he taught us about on the mountain called "Of the Olives" in Galilee.

And he said: "Peace be to you, my peace I give you!" And they all marveled and were afraid. The Savior laughed and said to them: "What are you thinking about? Are you perplexed? What are you searching for?" Philip said: "For the underlying reality of the universe and the plan."

—*The Sophia of Jesus Christ*

Those who say that the Lord died first and [then] rose up are in error, for he rose up first and [then] died. If one does not first attain the resurrection, he will not die.

—*The Gospel of Philip*

The twelve disciples were all sitting together and recalling what the Savior had said to each one of them, whether in secret or openly, and putting it in books—But I was writing that which was in my book—lo, the Savior appeared, after departing from us while we gazed after him. And five hundred and fifty days since he had risen from the dead, we said to him, "Have you departed and removed yourself from us?" But Jesus said, "No, but I shall go to the place from whence I came. If you wish to come with me, come!"

—*The Secret Book of James*

But it happened that after Jesus had risen from the dead He spent eleven years speaking with His disciples.

—*The Pistis Sophia*

Savior swallowed up death—[of this] you are not reckoned as being ignorant—for he put aside the world which is perishing. He transformed himself into an imperishable Aeon and raised himself up, having swallowed the visible by the invisible, and he gave us the way of our immortality. Then, indeed, as the Apostle said, "We suffered with him, and we arose with him, and we went to heaven with him." Now if we are manifest in this world wearing him, we are that one's beams, and we are embraced by him until our setting, that is to say, our death in this life. We are drawn to heaven by him, like beams by the sun, not being restrained by anything. This is the spiritual resurrection which swallows up the psychic in the same way as the fleshly.

But if there is one who does not believe, he does not have the [capacity to be] persuaded. For it is the domain of faith, my son, and not that which belongs to persuasion: the dead shall arise! There is one who believes among the philosophers who are in this world. At least he will arise. And let not the philosopher who is in this world have cause to believe that he is one who returns himself by himself—and [that] because of our faith! For we have known the Son of Man, and we have believed that he rose from among the dead. This is he of whom we say, "He became the destruction of death, as he is a great one in whom they believe." Great are those who believe.

. . .

What, then, is the resurrection? It is always the disclosure of those who have risen. For if you remember reading in the Gospel that Elijah appeared and Moses with him, do not think the resurrection is an illusion. It is no illusion, but it is truth! Indeed, it is more fitting to say the world is an illusion, rather than the resurrection which has come into being through our Lord the Savior, Jesus Christ.

But what am I telling you now? Those who are living shall die. How do they live in an illusion?

The rich have become poor, and the kings have been overthrown. Everything is prone to change. The world is an illusion!—lest, indeed, I rail at things to excess!

But the resurrection does not have this aforesaid character, for it is the truth which stands firm. It is the revelation of what is, and the transformation of things, and a transition into newness. For imperishability descends upon the perishable; the light flows down upon the darkness, swallowing it up; and the pleroma fills up the deficiency. These are the symbols and the images of the resurrection. He it is who makes the good.

Therefore, do not think in part, O Rheginos, nor live in conformity with this flesh for the sake of unanimity, but flee from the divisions and the fetters, and already you have the resurrection. For if he who will die knows about himself that he will die—even if he spends many years in this life, he is brought to this—why not consider yourself as risen and [already] brought to this? If you have the resurrection but continue as if you are to die—and yet that one knows that he has died—why, then, do I ignore your lack of exercise? It is fitting for each one to practice in a number of ways, and he shall be released from this Element that he may not fall into error but shall himself receive again what at first was.

—*The Treatise on the Resurrection*

BIBLIOGRAPHY

The Unauthorized Gospels

The Acts of John (from *The Apocryphal New Testament*)

The Acts of Peter (from *The Apocryphal New Testament*)

The Acts of Peter and the Twelve Apostles (from *The Nag Hammadi Library in English*)

The Acts of Thomas (from *The Apocryphal New Testament*)

The Apocalypse of Peter (from *The Nag Hammadi Library in English*)

The Arabic Infancy Gospel (from *The Ante-Nicene Fathers*)

The Assumption of the Virgin (from *The Apocryphal New Testament*)

The Book of John Concerning the Falling Asleep of Mary (from *The Ante-Nicene Fathers*)

The Book of St. Thomas the Contender (from *The Nag Hammadi Library in English*)

The Dialogue of the Savior (from *The Nag Hammadi Library in English*)

The Epistle of the Apostles (from *The Apocryphal New Testament*)

The First Apocalypse of James (from *The Nag Hammadi Library in English*)

The Gospel of Mary (from *The Nag Hammadi Library in English*)

The Gospel of Nicodemus (from *The Apocryphal New Testament*)

The Gospel of Peter (from *The Apocryphal New Testament*)

The Gospel of Philip (from *The Nag Hammadi Library in English*)

The Gospel of Pseudo-Matthew (from *The Ante-Nicene Fathers*)

The Gospel of Thomas (from *The Nag Hammadi Library in English*)

The Gospel of Truth (from *The Nag Hammadi Library in English*)

The History of Joseph the Carpenter (from *The Ante-Nicene Fathers*)

The Infancy Gospel of Thomas (from *The Apocryphal New Testament*)

The Manichaean Psalms of Heracleides (from *The Gospels of Mary*)

The Pistis Sophia (from *Pistis Sophia: A Gnostic Gospel*)

The Proto-Gospel of James (from *The Apocryphal New Testament*)

The Questions of Bartholomew (from *The Apocryphal New Testament*)

The Second Treatise of the Great Seth (from *The Nag Hammadi Library in English*)

The Secret Book of James (from *The Nag Hammadi Library in English*)

The Secret Book of John (from *The Nag Hammadi Library in English*)

The Sophia of Jesus Christ (from *The Nag Hammadi Library in English*)

The Treatise on the Resurrection (from *The Nag Hammadi Library in English*)

Sources

The Ante-Nicene Fathers: The Writings of the Fathers Down to A.D. 325, translated by Alexander Roberts, Wm. B. Eerdmans, Grand Rapids, Michigan, 1994.

The Apocryphal New Testament, translated by M. R. James, Clarendon Press, Oxford, 1924.

The Gospels of Mary: The Secret Tradition of Mary Magdalene, the Companion of Jesus, Marvin Meyer with Esther A. de Boer, HarperSanFrancisco, 2004.

The Nag Hammadi Library in English, James M. Robinson (ed.), 4th revised edition, E. J. Brill, Leiden, 1996.

Pistis Sophia: A Gnostic Gospel, translated by G. R. S. Mead, Spiritual Science Library, Garber Communications, Inc., New York, 1984.

Further Reading

Against Heresies, Ireneaus, A.D. 180.

Ancient Christian Gospels: Their History and Development, Helmut Koester, SCM Press, 1990.

Apocryphal Gospels: An Introduction, Hans-Josef Klauck, T. & T. Clark International, London and New York, 2003.

The Apocryphal Jesus: Legends of the Early Church, J. K. Elliott, Oxford University Press, Oxford, 1996.

Apologies, Justin Martyr, c. A.D. 150.

The Beginnings of Christianity: Essene Mystery, Gnostic Revelation and the Christian Vision, Andrew Welburn, Floris Books, Edinburgh, 2004.

Beyond Belief: The Secret Gospel of Thomas, Elaine Pagels, Vintage Books, New York, 2004.

The Da Vinci Code, Dan Brown, Doubleday, New York, 2003.

The Gnostic Discoveries: The Impact of the Nag Hammadi Library, Marvin Meyer, HarperSanFrancisco, 2005.

The Gnostic Gospels, Elaine Pagels, Weidenfeld and Nicolson, London, 1980.

The Gospel of Judas, edited by Rodolphe Kasser, Marvin Meyer, and Gregor Wurst, National Geographic, 2006.

Lost Scriptures, Bart D. Ehrman, Oxford University Press USA, New York, 2003.

The Secrets of Judas: The Story of the Misunderstood Disciple and His Lost Gospel, James M. Robinson, Harper SanFrancisco, 2006.

ABOUT THE EDITOR

Mian Ridge is a writer based in London. She studied theology at Oxford University. She has written for the *Financial Times*, the *Guardian*, the *Spectator*, and *The Tablet*.